DATE DUE

AP 7 '97			
NV 21 '07			
DE 19 '97			
DE 18 '98			
OC 11 '00			

DEMCO 38-296

THE SECOND HANDBOOK OF MINORITY STUDENT SERVICES

Edited by
Charles A. Taylor, Ph. D.

Published by
Praxis Publications, Inc.
2215 Atwood Ave.
Madison, WI 53704
(608) 244-5633

Library of Congress Cataloging-in-Publication Data

   The Second handbook of minority student services / edited by Charles A. Taylor
   p. cm.
   Includes bibliographical references
   ISBN 0-935483-13-6
   1. Minority college students--Services for--United States 2. Minority college students--United States--Societies, etc.
   I. Taylor, Charles A. (Charles Andrew)
   II. Handbook of minority student services
   LC3731.H225 1990   90-33779
   378.1'982--dc20   CIP

Praxis Publications, Inc. is an independent multi-cultural business enterprise that publishes educational and cultural literature and provides training programs, consultation and technical assistance to university and community groups. Praxis, headquartered in Madison, Wisconsin, is emerging as a leader in providing effective programs and services that seek to improve the quality of education for all people. We invite you to call or write us for additional information about our services and products.

Acknowledgements

Praxis Publications, Inc. gratefully acknowledges the following for their assistance in the completion of this book:

Colleen Carpenter, Tracy Dufour, Sheila Farrell, Patricia Hansen, Elizabeth Johanna, Mark McEahern, Londa Schuller, and Hazel Symonette.

Cover Design: Elizabeth Johanna

Dedication

This book is dedicated to students of color on college campuses. May it assist you in staying in school and graduating.

TABLE OF CONTENTS

TABLE OF CONTENTS

Chapter 4 Change and Empowerment

Appendices

FOREWORD

I'm extremely excited about this book and its potential to stimulate change and empowerment on your campus. Three years ago, we introduced the first *Handbook of Minority Student Services,* and the letters I received made it clear that many of you found creative and innovative ways to use it to your fullest advantage.

Enough of you asked when we planned to publish another handbook for us to once again assemble a team of top-notch experts in the area of student affairs.

Picking up where the first handbook left off, *The Second Handbook of Minority Student Services* is packed with information and programming ideas that will both improve services for students on your campus, as well as empower them to work for meaningful change.

Each chapter discusses a topic of import in depth, and provides examples of programs and models you can use. Information on student organizations, faculty involvement and special services is provided. We have devoted a full chapter to change and empowerment, because we believe that's what the academy should be about.

We've also dedicated this book to students of color who face increasing challenges at our institutions of higher education. With that in mind, our authors have provided a wealth of information that will be of value to students.

Mary Howard-Hamilton's *Ten Tenets* should be required reading for every African-American student on your campus. Louis Sarabia, director of Chicano Programs at New Mexico State University, shares ways to make student organizations effective. C. Scully Stikes provides a unique insight into the role faculty can play in retaining Minority students. Dr. Lamore Carter of Grambling discusses an academic skills model your campus may wish to emulate. Clinita Ford and Marvel Lang provide a persuasive argument in saying that we already know enough to improve Black student retention, while Forrest Toms offers a model for empowering students for diversity in the 90s. Other authors provide information that will help your students grow and succeed in an academic environment.

If you want to improve race relations on campus, set up effective programs for Minority students and empower students to work for change, then the *Second Handbook of Minority Student Services* is the place to start. As you read and implement the programs and ideas included in this book, keep in mind that helping students develop and grow is one of the most important tasks you can do for society.

Charles Taylor, editor

Making it Happen: Minority Student Organizations and Higher Education Institutional Responsibility

ABOUT THE AUTHOR:

Dr. Louis Sarabia

Dr. Louis Sarabia is Director of Chicano Programs at New Mexico State University. He received his B.A. from New Mexico Highlands University in 1965, in History and Political Science; his M.A. in 1970, also from NMHU; and his Ph.D. from the University of Santa Barbara in 1988, with a dissertation concerning the academic performance of Mexican-American students.

Dr. Sarabia has been a leader in establishing successful programs for Chicano students for over a decade. He has taught at the university level and has directed a variety of special services programs for students.

A popular speaker, Dr. Sarabia has addressed several educational conferences in the southwest, and gave the keynote lecture at both the Arizona Minority Student Services Conference and the New Mexico Quality Eucation Conference. Dr. Sarabia serves as a resource person on a number of issues related to Chicano concerns.

INTRODUCTION

Research has shown us that minority youth entering college often lack a clear idea why they are doing so; career goals are usually undefined. Since many are unsure exactly what a college degree will do to further a career, and since the definition of "career" is often at best a foreign idea, they do not feel as if they have lost something tangible when they drop out of school. Clearly, students need to be completely, not merely physically, integrated into campuses, if they are to feel that they will be missing something important should they leave. Involvement of students in organizations is one way to make the connection to campus more tangible and attractive.

The proportional increase of minority student presence in public education and on campuses is already evident; these students must be truly served by the educational system if this enrollment will make sense, both to the students and to the schools themselves. The economic survival of some schools in the southwest may depend on those schools' ability not only to matriculate, but to retain and graduate, minority students.

The author examines factors which must be considered if the administration of a college is to successfully encourage minority students to involve themselves in their campus via membership in student organizations. Intra-minority demographic group differences, within-group differences in attitude toward status as a minority, the type of campus, and the potential for peer-group and student mentor support is examined. Also examined are the important attributes of the staff sponsor for any group, and possible group activities to consider. Finally, a case study is made of the *Associated Hispanic Students* organization at New Mexico State University.

MAKING IT HAPPEN:

Minority Student Organizations and Higher Education Institutional Responsibility

by
Dr. Louis Sarabia

The mission statement for minority student programs and services in the Council for Advancement of Standards and Guidelines for Student Services/Development Programs (CAS) states that:

> The provision of minority student programs and services should presuppose a strong campus sense of a common community, serving all its citizens fairly, and marked in the main by:
> access to, rather than exclusion from, academic, social, and recreational groups and activities;
> shared goals;
> intentional social intercourse, rather than passive social isolation or active social exclusion; and
> integration rather than segregation (1986).

The CAS guidelines are interesting in that "a strong sense of common community" and "shared goals" are presupposed. The CAS guidelines indicate that the institution's goals should also be "shared" by the majority of the students, staff, and faculty.

For minority youth, this may be a problem. Minority youngsters are often the first in their family to attend college. While the institution may have a mission statement, the minority student may not know what it is.

Research suggests that more often than not, minority youth have very unclear career goals. They are not sure what higher education can do for their future because they have no idea what that future may be. In a great many cases, they aren't really sure why they are in college at all. So, the ideals of "shared goals" and "sense of community" often do not apply to minority students.

Factors Affecting Organizations

Minority students often find organizations useful in coping with a world they do not fully comprehend, and which they may perceive as hostile and uninviting. Student organizations can have many functions.

The type and effectiveness of a student organization on a particular campus is dependent on a number of factors:

First, the number of minority students on a campus will have an effect on the type of organizations formed and the number of organizations.

Second, for some students, an organization may serve as a means for exploring a non-academic interest. For others, organizations often serve to strengthen religious beliefs. Still others use organizations for social or political purposes.

Third, the function of a student organization will also be affected by the "level of ethnicity" of the student. That is, some students feel very strongly about "being" a minority; others resent being considered a minority, and yet other students will accept the minority label if it means getting a tutor or scholarship.

A fourth factor that will determine the form and function of the organization is the sponsor. The sponsor's commitment to minority students, to the institution, and to his or her profession will often determine the success or failure of an organization. While the students may be willing and eager, if the organization has weak leadership it will have poor vision and poor continuity.

Regardless of the type of school, the number of students, or the motivation of the students, minority student organizations have been, and will continue to be, important in the overall educational success of minority youth.

The Demographic Realities: Beginning about ten years ago, demographers began to speak of a "minority-majority shift" in the population of our nation's schools and colleges. In the public schools of the southwest, increases in the number of minority students, accompanied by decreases in the number of white students, have already begun to occur. The Los Angeles public schools now enroll more minority students than white students.

Seventy-five percent of the children who began kindergarten in New Mexico in 1988 were minority children.

This trend suggests that within the next ten to fifteen years, many of our nation's colleges and universities will be enrolling more minority students than ever before. For schools in the southwest particularly, the enrollment of minority students and the successful retention of those students may mean economic survival.

Also at issue is the economic survival of our nation. It is expected that by the year 2000, minorities will comprise one-third of our nation's work force. Educating that minority population will be crucial to the economic growth and stability of the United States.

In 1986, the Hispanic Association of Colleges and Universities (HACU) was organized with membership limited to institutions having at least twenty-five percent Hispanic student enrollment. The limit was set, according to the leadership of HACU, because it represents a critical mass—a proportion whose presence on campus cannot be ignored, even requiring that changes be made in the hiring policies of the institution.

The presence of high proportions of minority students on campus will require that the social structure of the institution be modified. An institution with a twenty-five percent minority enrollment will no longer be able to rely exclusively on an office of minority affairs to provide services to minority students. Instead it will have to recognize the fact that all offices and all aspects of campus life will be affected by the sheer number of minority students enrolled in the institution.

Intra-Minority Group Differences: While non-minority faculty and staff may recognize the importance of having minority student organizations on their campuses, they should also be aware that minority students are not all alike. A Black student from Houston is as different from a Black student from Albuquerque as a white student from the rural south is different from a white student from the Bronx. American Indian students from urban areas are not the same as American Indians who grew up on a reservation and went to boarding schools. Consequently, minority students cannot be treated as if they had the same mind set. Non-minorities often fail to realize basic with-in group differences, but these differences cannot be ignored.

Another problem often encountered on campuses that have a multi-ethnic/multi-cultural enrollment is that minority students, whether Hispanic, American Indian or Black, are perceived by non-minorities as sharing similar lifestyles and aspirations. This is simply not so. Often, in fact, minority students have had less contact with other minority students than with white students, and the interactions of minority students with one another are often strained. As a result, when a non-minority group member suggests, often with good intentions, that small minority organizations merge, the advice is rejected and the non-minority loses credibility with minority students.

With-in Group Differences: There is also the question of minority students' self-perception. Many minority students have grown up in communities where their minority status was extremely obvious. They view themselves as a minority and this perception may have either negative or positive results. These minority students may feel they are inferior, that their ethnicity is a drawback, and that they should disassociate themselves from their "minority status."

Other students, however, come from communities where they are in the majority. The mayor and city council are racial minorities, the school superintendent is a minority, their teachers and counselors were minorities. The perception of being a minority, to these students, is quite different from that of the first group of students. These students will often view their minority status neutrally. They just don't think too much about it one way or the other. They have a good sense of who and what they are. They don't have to prove themselves to anyone; nor are they ashamed of who they are.

Campus Type-Predominantly Non-Minority: The question of access is a different matter. On a campus with an enrollment of several thousand students and a minority population of one or two hundred, access to academic, social and recreational activities is extremely important. In such cases, minority student organizations may parallel organizations designed for the majority group population. Often the presence of minority student organizations may cause misunderstanding among non-minorities.

For example, minority groups may organize and sponsor their own intramural athletic teams. On many campuses, minority student organizations are instrumental in the recruitment efforts of the institution, and also provide their own, separate, orientation programs for incoming students. They function as a network on campus, with the minority services office serving as a gathering place and resource center.

The parallel nature of these organizations can, and usually does, cause antagonism among non-minority students and staff. Why should there be separate minority student volleyball or basketball teams? Why can't these students join teams that already exist? Aren't these organizations and their members being separatist? These are the questions sponsors of these groups are going to face. The success of minority student organizations is often dependent on non-minority faculty and staff perception of the organizations.

The answer, of course, is that on campuses with very small minority student populations, many minority students will not participate in any activity if they have no choice other than already established groups. They will not feel the organization is theirs, and ownership is key to belonging. Being the only "different" student in a group can be intimidating--participation will be limited by the feeling that they are outsiders.

Minority student organizations can serve to help the minority student find his or her way. Minority group organizations often rely heavily on the leadership of upperclass students to provide a big brother/big sister atmosphere. The older students encourage, cajole, criticize, hug and scold. The function of the minority student organization, in many instances, is to replace the family left behind.

Minority youth will often find acceptance in this group, not because of the school from which they graduated, not because of their wealth, or lack of it, not because of their grades, but because of who they are. Non-minority faculty and staff who recognize and support these important facets of minority student organizations can do much to guarantee the success of these organizations on their campuses.

Minority student organizations are much easier to build and nurture on campuses where minorities are really in the minority than on campuses with large minority student populations. With a small number of minority students, the sponsor can get to know most of the students. Their small numbers also make it possible for the minority students to know each other. Most of the minority students will attend at least a few of the meetings held, primarily because "it's the only show in town."

It is imperative that such an organization have a strong, committed, empathetic sponsor. The sponsor will serve a parental role in the organization, and it is vital that he/she attend every meeting.

The sponsor should be seen by the students, as well as by the institution, as someone who is knowledgeable and to be respected. The sponsor will be the key to the success or failure of such an organization on a predominantly non-minority campus.

Campus Type--Minority Serving Institution: On a campus with a large minority student population, the number of minority students dictates that they be involved in all aspects of campus life, from dorm activities, to fraternities, to political and religious groups. The options for minority students to participate in campus life are more numerous for these students than for students on campuses having smaller numbers of minority students. Thus, minority student organizations have to be different.

Students should be encouraged to interact with the institution on their own terms and for their own interests. They should be encouraged to put forth candidates for the student government. They should be encouraged to serve on speaker committees, homecoming planning committees, film selection committees, etc. Their participation should not be taken lightly. This means that students selected to serve on university committees should attend all meetings, and should be prepared to offer well thought out alternatives when they disagree with the majority of the committee. The role of the sponsor in selecting and assisting these students to participate in these activities is vital.

Sponsorship: Having shown how important the sponsor of a minority student organization is, let us turn our attention to this position. Ideally, the sponsor should be a member of a minority group, and more importantly, identify with the minority group. Many faculty and staff, even though they are minorities, do not see such group membership as being important. They see themselves as having overcome their ethnicity. They often resent being categorized as minority group members. They see themselves as professionals, not as minority professionals. Sometimes they view minority staff members who are involved in minority services as "professional minorities." Their attitude simply will not allow them to work effectively as sponsors of minority student organizatons.

In addition, the faculty or staff sponsor should have an above average understanding of the internal workings of the institution. Students are often going to suggest activities that run counter to institutional policy. The sponsor has to recognize these situations and head them off in such a way that his or her credibility with the group is not damaged. Very seldom will a first year member of the faculty or staff have the knowledge necessary to be a good sponsor, especially if he or she must work alone in this capacity.

On a campus where the minority student presence is substantial, the student group sponsor must know something about everything. It would be nice, if on this type of campus, there were more ethnic/racial minority faculty and staff members to assist in advising and sponsoring student organizations, but this will rarely be the case. Most of the time minority student organizations are going to be sponsored by the staff of the minority services office.

Activities

Social: All meetings should involve some type of social activity. Usually, socializing can take place after a meeting. The social activity may take place on or off campus, depending on the location of the campus and transportation. It may take place in a public place or a private home. Going out for a pizza is a good way to get students involved in an organization, and also gives the sponsor a chance to see the students in an off-campus, out-of-class environment. The social activities also give the students a chance to see their sponsor in an out-of-office, casual situation.

Caution should be exercised regarding availability of alcohol at student gatherings. A great deal of concern has been expressed in the past few years about alcohol and students. Anytime alcohol is present, student advisors should be extremely vigilant.

Often, students who do not ordinarily participate will show up because of the availability of free booze. Also, complying with laws on the drinking age is almost impossible. Alcohol can bring out the worst in people, and a great deal of time is spent trying to prevent fights and keep the furniture intact. The possibility of lawsuits is another a major consideration.

Community: Community activities are popular among many student groups. However, depending on the type of community in which the campus is located, this may be a problem. If the community is predominantly white, there may not be a minority community with which to interact. Also, if the minority students are recruited from other areas of the state or nation, they may feel no sense of belonging and it may be difficult to involve them within the larger community's life. Organized student activities in such communities should be "neutral" in nature, such as participation in a food drive benefiting a homeless shelter. In this case, the results of the activity is more important than who is involved. This type of activity can orient the students to the community in which they will be living for the next few years, and can introduce them to others within the community.

Cultural: All efforts should be made to insure that cultural activities, regardless of type, are open to the entire campus and local community. Cultural activities may include films, speakers, dance and theatre groups, musicians, art shows, folklife and folk art exhibits.

The key to cultural programming is funding, and minority student organizations should have access to funds. These funds should be made available through the minority services office, the University's speakers' committee, museum or art gallery funding, or through the student government.

The minority organization and its sponsor should integrate minority programming and activities into all segments of campus life. If the English department is having a poetry reading, are some of the invited poets minorities? If the art department is featuring regional artists, are minorities included? Has the History department considered a minority as a distinguished visiting professor?

Orientation: Experience has shown that students are often the best source of information regarding what it takes to survive and to be successful academically. Veteran students can be recruited by involving the minority student organization in planning orientation for new students. These older students can help determine what information is vital and when that information should be shared. Orientation is not a one-time event; it continues throughout the year as new concerns or needs are raised. By scheduling discussion meetings between veteran and new students, students can deal directly with issues they define as important. Students participate more readily if the issues or discussion topics are theirs. New students also tend to accept advice from other students more readily than from establishment types.

Leadership Development: Student organizations also provide leadership training. Generally, board meetings with student officers can be held prior to regular membership meetings.

These meetings should orient the officers to the purpose of the organization, the role of the sponsors, rules and regulations regarding student organizations on campus, and who's who at the university. These meetings may include discussion of how the university is structured, the functions of the various vice presidents, deans, department heads, and student support services offices as well as where they are located.

The officers and sponsors should work on developing an agenda for the next meeting. The agenda should be used to keep things moving smoothly, to provide information, and to encourage participation. The agenda format can usually be a simple outline updating the group on past activities, seeking suggestions for future activities, and providing information about minority services and university activities which might be of interest to our students. Additionally, students may be assisted in learning strategies for handling a disruptive member, the art of compromise, and how to say no without antagonizing. These skills will be important in the student's life both in and after college.

Hispanic Organizations on Campus: A Case Study

On a campus where Hispanic students comprise over 28 percent of the student enrollment, there is great access to academic and social groups and activities. Hispanic students are represented in most fraternities, sororities, the student government, and a large number of student organizations, including professional and honorary groups.

General Interest: Our oldest Hispanic student organization is the *Associated Hispanic Students* (AHS), formerly known as *Los Chicanos de NMSU*. This group started as an activist organization. Its name change reflects a change in student attitudes, particularly the perception by some Hispanic students that the term "Chicano" is too radical.

Beginning in 1971, AHS successfully lobbied for the establishment of ethnic studies programs, for more Chicano faculty and staff, and for the establishment of ethnic offices. AHS also convinced the University to include course content which reflects a multi-cultural state and university, and was responsible for more minority participation in student government elections and activities.

In addition to pushing for a greater voice in campus activities, AHS has also committed a large amount of time to community activities. Students have participated in the Big Brother/Big Sister program, the Salvation Army's youth program, and have worked with Special Olympics. They have gone caroling (in Spanish) to senior citizens' centers, collected food for local food banks, participated in blood drives, and assisted in city clean-up and beautification programs.

The major annual events for AHS have included building a float for the Homecoming parade, sponsoring Chicano Week (a series of activities including speakers, art shows, car shows, a fashion show, movies, and dances). In addition, AHS has been involved in hosting three major conferences, each with more than 400 participants from throughout the state and nation.

Professional Organizations: The emergence and development of professionally oriented student organizations is about ten years old. They have spawned a number of national professional organizations. Today there are two major Hispanic engineering societies, a newly formed Hispanic MBA group, and several groups for Hispanic Certified Public Accountants. Other groups of professionals will emerge as students participate in career-oriented organizations on campus and seek similar groups in the world of work.

On our campus we have three professional organizations: the Society of Hispanic Professional Engineers, the Hispanic Business Organization, and the Hispanic Educators Association. These three groups share some functional similarities in that they serve a specific minority population and their activities are geared toward career development and community involvement.

An example is the Society of Hispanic Professional Engineers, (SHPE), a professional organization whose members are majoring in engineering, computer science, mathematics and physics. It was founded and sponsored by the Chicano Programs Office in 1976. Officers are president, a president-elect, a secretary and treasurer, and approximately ten committee chairs. The president is, according to by-laws, a senior. The president-elect functions as a vice-president, and must be a junior when elected. This system provides for mature leadership, experience in a leadership role prior to assuming the presidency, and a close working relationship between the top officers.

As a professional organization, SHPE strives to provide opportunities for professional development. It keeps students informed of upcoming recruitment visits, helps plan and publicize career fairs, prepares resume booklets, has a representative on the Engineering Council, and provides tutorial assistance to its members. SPHE has also been involved in a number of community activities, such as installing wheelchair ramps and handrails at the homes of disabled citizens.

Conclusion

Our campus has a large, varied, Hispanic population. We have students from seventh generation families and students who were born in Mexico. Some of our students are the first in their families to attend college; some are from a line of parents and grandparents who attended college. We have students who know as freshmen what medical school they will attend, while others just took their GED exam two days ago.

We have found that the key element in having successful and active student organizations is hard work--by the institution, by the students, and by the sponsors. As our student populations change, so must our organizations. By changing, our organizations remain fresh, active, and alive.

Ten Ways to Keep Members Involved
In Your Student Organization Year Round

ABOUT THE AUTHOR:

Dr. Charles
Taylor

Charles Taylor is currently the publisher and president of Praxis Publications, Inc., a publishing firm that publishes books and a wide range of literature pertaining to Minority Student Services. Dr. Taylor earned his Ph. D. at the University of Wisconsin-Madison in Curriculum and Instruction with an emphasis on Educational Technology. He earned his Masters in Education from the University of Oregon and his B.S. from Southeast Missouri State University. He has been involved in student services for over fifteen years.

Charles has served as an Acting Assistant Vice Chancellor for Academic Support Services, director of a TRIO program (TRIO programs are special services programs funded by the Department of Education), director of a Multicultural Education Center, as an academic advisor, financial aid officer and as an administrator in the second largest school district in Wisconsin during his illustrious career. He has served as an advisor to many student

organizations and is founder of Wisconsin's annual Minority High School Student Leadership Conference. He continues to serve as a consultant to college campuses throughout America in the area of Minority Student Services.

In addition to Dr. Taylor's education mission, he has a service mission to independent publishers of color. Charles is founder of the Minority Publishers Exchange, a national network of Minority Publishers, editor of its newsletter and publisher of its annual catalog. He is fast becoming recognized as a dynamic leader in the independent publishing movement.

TEN WAYS TO KEEP MEMBERS INVOLVED

In Your Student Organization Year Round

by
Dr. Charles
Taylor

While working with and observing student groups across the country, I've picked up some successful strategies to help you keep students interested in your organizations. Below I've briefly described ten of the best. If you implement these strategies consistently, you should experience a great deal of success.

1. DISTRIBUTE your minutes to those who are present, but especially to those who are absent. Send minutes to your advisor, your funding source, professors and administrators who support you or from whom you are seeking support. This one little practice of distributing your minutes will have tremendous pay-off at the end of the year. The minutes that you distribute to students should include a record of who was present and who was absent. When students get a copy of the minutes with their names listed under absent, they'll know they were not only missed but expected to be there. When they see their names showing up on the absent list week after week, eventually they'll start to attend.

2. INVOLVE all of your members in the organization so they feel a part of it. If there is a perception that a few people make all the decisions and that other's opinions won't matter, then it becomes more difficult to sustain student interest in the organization. Take a real hard look at your committee structure. Decide the purpose of each committee. Determine if the committee is really needed and if so, is it really fulfilling its mission. If not, consider revising its mission so that everyone is clear on what is expected. Ask yourself if commit-tees have proven to be the best method to sustain member involvement.

3. SURVEY your membership. Find out what their priorities and interests really are. Is the time and date you're meeting the best time for most members? Your survey should help determine that.

4. EVALUATE your organization. Find out the

top two reasons why members don't come and don't participate. Do they know in advance what's going to be on the agenda? Who determines how the funds are spent? Who determines what programs are offered? Can any member bring an agenda item to the meeting? Does your organization really reflect the wishes of its members or the wishes of its leadership? When you evaluate every aspect of your organization you have to ask these tough questions.

5. ASSIGN responsibilities by month. To sustain year long involvement and to get various students to work together, designate each month or every other month to certain members. For example, freshmen and junior members can plan activities for April while sophomores and seniors do May; or females plan October's activities while males plan November's, etc.

6. FOLLOW UP with phone calls after the meeting. Normally organizations call members before the meeting starts, asking them whether they plan on attending or not. Well, try a little reverse psychology. After each meeting, call those who were absent. Callers should inform the absentees that they missed an important meeting and that their presence is needed at the next meeting so that your organization's work can continue.

7. HAVE EACH ONE BRING ONE. Challenge each member to bring someone from the absent list to the next meeting. Then provide some type of acknowledgment each month by recognizing the person who has brought the most members each month.

8. DEVELOP incentives. Everyone likes group activities. Sponsor activities for the group to participate in either before or after the meeting so people look forward to attending. Reduce dues by 10% for good attendance or for students who make the Dean's list, etc...

9. PROVIDE confidential information. At each meeting try to have an important announcement, or news that they can only get by attending the meetings. You can mention this information in your minutes under confidential message but don't describe it. Let students know your meetings are very important and when they miss, they are missing out on valuable information.

10. EXPERIMENT, Experiment, Experiment! Don't give up! Don't expect change overnight. Try new approaches and new ways to involve members, such as the following:

a) For freshmen students, try sending their parents a letter introducing your organization and asking parents to encourage their children to get involved with it.

b) Have your public affairs office send out press releases about students in your organization to their hometown newspapers. There is nothing more motivating than good publicity.

c) Try to get your organization featured regularly in your campus's newspaper.

d) Publish a 1-2 page newsletter about your organization's members, activities etc. and circulate to all members and interested parties including students' parents.

Remember, change takes place slowly, but if you begin to implement each of these ideas and others that you may come up with, you will experience greater involvement within your organization.

Establishing Effective Activities:
for Minority Students on Campus

ABOUT THE AUTHOR:

Dr. K. Paul Kasambira

Dr. K. Paul Kasambira is Associate Professor of Education and Director of Minority Student Services at Bradley University, Peoria, Illinois. Dr. Kasambira received his T.I., an undergraduate teaching degree, from Gwelo Teacher's College, Zimbabwe, Africa, in 1967; his B.A. from Taylor University, Upland, Indiana, in English and Religious Studies, in 1975; his M.A. from Ball State University, Muncie, Indiana, in Secondary Teacher Education and Educational Psychology, in 1976; and his Ed.D., also from Ball State, in Secondary Teacher Education, Pre-Counseling Psychology, and Curriculum Development, in 1979. Dr. Kasambira is licensed by the National Board of Certified Counselors. He has co-authored a textbook and has had numerous articles published in the United States, Canada, and Africa.

Dr. Kasambira conducts presentations to student affairs, teacher education, religious, minority, college, and university audiences at the state, national, and international levels. He does consulting work on a variety of topics related to minority student services.

INTRODUCTION

There is a lack of comprehensive research data available in the public domain today dealing directly with minorities on predominantly white campuses. This article attempts to address that need in part by presenting a compilation of research data which does exist and which has helped the author in his position as Minority Student Services Director. The author takes a look at special programs available to minority students on majority campuses. He describes the alternative campus program at Mount St. Mary's College in Los Angeles, recruitment and retention efforts at Glendale Community College in Arizona, the Peer Information Counseling program in place at the university library in Ann Arbor, Michigan, and elements of the program in place at Bradley University. A review of the research thus far is presented, and factors associated with retention and attrition are delineated.

The author presents elements that he feels are essential to the development and implementation of effective minority students services on campus. He describes several events on the Bradley minority student services' calendar, how they are organized by students and faculty each year, and why they are important to the minority students there.

ESTABLISHING EFFECTIVE ACTIVITIES

For Minority Students on Campus

by
Dr. K. Paul
Kasambira

As institutions of higher education become less financially healthy, certain programs that some people consider "peripheral," "burdensome," or "insignificant," will continue to suffer. On some university campuses, programs such as Black Studies, Minority Services and International Student Services are not on the central administration's priority lists. Invariably, directors of these programs have to "fight" for financial support and justify the existence of their programs. This on-going battle in which the directors are forced to engage weakens the effectiveness of the services being delivered to minority populations.

As a practitioner in this area, my sincere advice to those directors who find themselves in this predicament is that they should use it as an opportunity to deliver effective activities to the minority students they serve. If minority programs and services are successful they will less likely fall prey to budget cuts. This is not an easy task, but this chapter is intended to give you, the practitioner, some pointers concerning what you can do to deliver those services effectively.

Minorities: A Definition

Perhaps one point that should be emphasized is to be aware of how the term minority is defined on your campus. For a long time Native Americans and Blacks were the only minorities referred to in this country. After the world wars, other ethnic groups came to America from Europe, the Caribbean Islands, the Dominican Republic, Cuba, Asia, Central America, South America and Africa. This is further complicated by the fact that I am addressing the term "minority" in academe. There is a growing group comprised of non-traditional students: students who are married with children, returning adult students, and any other "non-traditional" students past the age of twenty-five. Should this group be considered a minority? And what about women, or people with limiting

physical disabilities? People whose sexual preference or orientation is different from the norm?
Are they to be considered a minority as well? For
the purpose of this article I've adopted the definition used by most Federal agencies. A person is a
minority if he or she falls within one of the
following categories:

A. American Indian and Alaska Native -
   This includes American Indians and Alaskan
   Aluets, Eskimos or Indians. A person having
   origins in any of the original peoples of North
   America who maintains cultural identification
   through affiliation or community recognition.

B. Asian or Pacific Islander -
   A person having origins in any of the original
   peoples of Southeast Asia, the Indian
   subcontinent or the Pacific Islands.

C. Black and African-American -
   A person having origins in any of the Black
   racial groups of Africa.

D. Hispanic -
   A person of Mexican, Puerto Rican, Cuban,
   Central, South American or other Spanish
   culture or origin, regardless of race.
                                     (Calvert, 1975)

A good addition to this list would be "other" which
would include people of mixed racial parentages.

Along with the problem of deciding who is
included in this group defined "minority," the term
itself denotes a small portion of the population.
This is misleading. According to the 1988
Statistical Abstract of the United States, between
1961 and 1985 over nine million people immi-
grated from Mexico, the Caribbean Islands, the
Dominican Republic, Cuba, Asia, Central America,
South America and Africa. Furthermore, trends
indicate that sixty percent of the labor force will
be made up of minority workers in the 21st
century.

Problematically, statistics indicate that 70

percent of Hispanic students and 28 percent of
Black students drop out of high school (Nunez-
Wormack, Elsa, 1989).

Research and Minority Programming

Developing successful programs requires
research and assessment of programs already
existing. Unfortunately, there is very little
research. Research of minorities in predominantly
white institutions of higher education did not
appear until the late 1970s. In preparing material
for this article, the author wrote or called a
variety of agencies with the hope of acquiring
data, but many of them did not yield much information. The most productive source was the
Educational Resources Information Center
(ERIC). Nevertheless, the related research
included here is intended to be helpful to you in
establishing minority programs.

Research

Cervantes and Oscar (1988) discovered several
factors associated with academic underachievement
and high attrition of minority students. Most
critical are:

(1) self-esteem and self-concept;

(2) educational barriers; and

(3) systematic issues such as biased tests, poverty,
    discrimination, and alienation in schools.

Their recommendations to improve this situation
include: making legislative changes at all levels;
providing greater financial aid to underrepresented
minorities; and improving congruency (the match
or fit between the needs, interests and skills of the
individual and those of the communities of the
institution). According to Cervantes and Oscar, it is
important for faculty and administrators to work
together in remedial academic programs; academic
advising; personal, financial and career counseling;

and minority support groups. Minority staffing is important as it offers role models. New criteria should be developed to predict college success for the minority student, as criteria used for Caucasian students may be inappropriate. Universities should implement programs and activities which would increase interaction between minority and Euro-American students.

In a paper presented by Janet Smith (1988) at the Annual Convention of the Association of Community College Trustees, efforts to enhance minority recruitment, retention and achievement included:

(1) the strategies that are part of an overall plan for institutional advancement;

(2) cooperative relationships that are developed with urban high schools and 4-year institutions;

(3) a sound theoretical framework governing the development of efforts at change; and

(4) clearly defined structural relationships and accountabilities within the staff.

Indeed, these imperatives are in operation at the Cuyahoga Community College in its Greater Cleveland Area Urban Demonstration Laboratory Model. Here access and retention are seen as touchstones for institutional advancement. "Bridge" programs of learning and support services are being developed; and the "effective school theory" is the basis for organizing and assessing programmatic efforts. Clearly defined operational responsibilities have been established (Smith, 1988).

In 1988, in response to a Board of Regents request, a task force was established to study minority student recruitment, admission, and retention in the University of Nevada System.

Representatives from all campuses compiled data on minority student participation in postsecondary education and on programs aimed exclusively at minority students. They met with representatives of Black, Hispanic, Asian, and American Indian groups throughout the state. Their findings:

Between 1980 and 1988 the minority proportion of the Nevada population increased 2.2%;

Between 1982 to 1988 the proportion of minority school-age children grew 2.6%;

Minority high school graduation rates are lower than those of Whites;

A smaller proportion of minority group members than Whites attended four years of college (with the exception of Asians); and

Although state university minority enrollments peaked in 1985, they still represented a smaller proportion of the minority community than othe corresponding proportions for the White community.

Recommendations by the task force included:

a written policy endorsing and encouraging minority student recruitment, admission, and retention;

institutional responsibility for support of minority recruitment and retention programs;

a minority grants-in-aid program;

and continued task force efforts.
(Minority Outreach Task Force, 1988)

Clewell studied institutional practices of retaining minorities at four institutions: Boston College, California State University at Fresno, University of North Carolina at Greensboro, and Purdue University Minority Engineering Program. These four-year, "white" institutions were chosen because they demonstrated good retention rates of minorities. The researchers concluded that some of the reasons for the success of these programs included motivating students to aspire to higher education, preparing them for the rigors of a college career, assisting them to matriculate, helping them finance their education, and offering academic and personal support during their college years (Clewell, 1986).

In 1986, Genevieve Ramirez conducted a study examining the characteristics, needs, and actual experiences of Latino (Mexican American/ Chicano and other Hispanic) students enrolled at California State University, Long Beach (CSULB). Resources included: university records showing Hispanic demographic characteristics; comparison of Student Affirmative Action Outreach Program (SAA) participants with non-participant Latino peers, and random sample interviews with SAA participants. Though Latino CSULB enrollment grew from 5.4% to 8.7% from 1975 to 1985, Latinos, who comprised 19.1% of California high school graduates, were greatly underrepresented. Of SAA Latino students entering CSULB in 1982-83, 73% had been retained to begin their fourth year in 1985 or had graduated. The study indicated academic failure/difficulty results from:

unrealistic expectations,

lack of clear personal goals deemed attainable,

general alienation from the institutional mainstream, and

interference of external circumstances.

Factors favoring academic persistence/performance include:

parental influence,

early expectations for higher education,

appropriate course scheduling incorporating skills development classes with academic solids,

and clear career/major direction.
(Ramirez, 1986)

This research could prove to be a valuable tool for setting up minority programs on campuses across the country. Along with this research a closer look at programs already existing can provide ideas for setting up more effective programs.

Programs

One of the oldest and most effective programs specifically designed to retain ethnically diverse students can be found at Mount St. Mary's College in Los Angeles, California. In 1960, MSMC opened the Doheny campus as an alternative for students who had potential for college, but who were not eligible to enter MSMCs traditional baccalaureate degree programs at the main campus. The Doheny program has enabled many students to complete associate in arts and baccalaureate degrees at the main campus.

The success of the retention program at MSMC is attributed to a coordinated program of academic development and support services. It involves the following components:

(1) admissions and testing to assess skill levels and potential for success;

(2) required classes to develop skills in areas where testing shows students are weak;

(3) an extended, semester-long orientation course;

(4) required work with a tutor at the Learning Resource Center;

(5) an early warning system to notify students and their advisors of any difficulties the students are having;

(6) a residence program capable of housing as many as 170 students;

(7) availability of courses in community outreach;

(8) an English as a Second Language course; and

(9) multicutural tools and services.

The MSMC program is based on the belief that students can succeed in college if placed in a supportive environment where there is individual attention, intervention when difficulties appear, and feedback from the faculty and administration (Kelly, 1960).

At the University of Michigan in Ann Arbor a program was developed to address the problem of declining enrollment and graduation rates of minority students. The program, called Peer Information Counseling (PIC), is intended to help minority students use the university library effectively. The main goals of this program are:

furthering the use of the library and of microcomputers by minority students;

improving the information-handling skills and computer skills of minority students,

developing the information-handling, computer, and counseling skills of the students hired as counselors; and

contributing to a campus atmosphere which promotes retention of minority undergraduates.

In this program, minority students are identified and hired by the university library to serve in the following general capacities:

assisting patrons at the reference desk,

tutoring students in word processing,

providing in-depth term paper assistance,

producing instructional materials, and

publicizing the PIC program.

The hired PIC counselors are trained in both basic reference skills and effective public service. They are also trained in working at the reference desk, as well as working with minority students who need help with research papers or the use of computers (MacAdam and Nichols, 1989).

At Glendale Community College in Arizona, Mendoza (1988) developed a microcomputer tracking system to enhance minority recruitment and retention. In the report describing the system, introductory sections offer a rationale for minority emphasis programs, define the term "minority," enumerate reasons for attending a community college, and examine the objectives and implementation of minority emphasis programs. The following sections focus on:

(1) educational outreach and recruitment;

(2) retention services;

(3) an early warning system whereby students in academic difficulty are referred to appropriate services; and

(4) a student information system (SIS), which centralizes registration, transcripts, class rosters, enrollment reports, and financial aid data.

The final sections look at the SIS in greater detail, examining system development, downloading capabilities, data retrieval, and features which permit the college to contact targeted groups, including unregistered applicants, dropouts, and new students. The database tracking system uses information downloaded from the SIS to track Hispanic, Black, American Indian, and Asian/Pacific Islander student enrollments and progress (Mendoza, 1988).

Developing a Survey Instrument to Establish Effective Programs

Establishing effective activities for minorities on a predominantly white campus does not just happen. Careful planning must be done based on students' needs. Identifying those needs is vital to the success of a program.

Systematic data collection must be done and this information should be shared with all interested parties and ultimately requires commitment or cooperation from all units on campus. A research or survey instrument must be used to assess the students' needs. The instrument I have used at Bradley University, Peoria, Illinois has been used in several universities since its appearance in the first *Handbook of Minority Student Services,* published in 1986 by Praxis

Publications, Inc. The general categories in that survey instrument, I believe, are necessary components and should be included in any needs assessment you might conduct. These categories are listed below.

Category 1 - Demographic Information

This category includes information of a demographic nature such as the respondents' sex (male or female) and their classification in college (freshman, sophomore, junior, senior or graduate standing). Respondents should also state whether or not they are transfer students or students-at-large. This is important because researchers might want to collaborate the respondents' answers with variables such as sex and year classification with their major or another variable. It may be, for example, important to know how many females or males responded to the survey.

Category 2 - Housing/Accommodations

This category requests information about the students' housing: whether they live on or off campus, in an apartment, at home with their family, in a Greek house, or in another type of housing arrangement. Accommodation is likely to be connected with the students' response to items in the rest of the categories in the survey instrument and may have a bearing on the students' particular needs.

Category 3 - Decision Factors

This section covers items that have to do with decision factors, particularly with the best days or times the respondent might feel would be convenient for him/her to attend campus activities. An office, unit, or institution might have a magnificent program slated to take place when most students are in class or otherwise occupied, and so this situation or activity would draw only a handful of people. This not only limits the number who could benefit by attendance, it is not cost effective.

Category 4 - Information and Communication

This category can reveal the best means that an institution could use to effectively communicate with students. Options to be indicated by the respondents include the college/university newspaper, radio or television station, posters, newsletters, mailboxes, and minority organization advisory council representatives. It is critical for planning a program to know how to reach the students.

Category 5 - Participation in Activities

This section would offer a list of possible activities respondents might like to participate in, such as exhibits, movies, dances, lectures/speakers, theatrical performances, concerts, sports events, or other similar activities. There would be no point in sponsoring an event if few students would attend.

Category 6 - Types of Music

This is more specific than category 5 as it deals exclusively with the specific kinds of music respondents favor. Options may range from soul music and rock 'n' roll to folk, classical, jazz, reggae, disco, and country music.

Category 7 - Movies/Films

This category gives the respondents an opportunity to indicate what kind of movies or films they would like to see on campus. This might include science fiction films, horror films, musicals, westerns, mystery films or documentaries.

Category 8 - Speaker/Lecturer Preference

Here the respondents are expected to indicate their preferences of speaker/lecture presentations. The options here might include, but should not be restricted to, political, cultural, international, scientific, academic, minority, religious, or current event issues.

Category 9 - Activity/Interest Profile

This category would include options dealing with the respondents' activity/interest profiles. In simple terms, the category solicits the respondents' opinion on activity preferences. These preferences might include participation in college or university political activities (student council, government, or senate); intramural sports; professional; honorary; or social fraternities or sororities; student alliances; religious groups; athletic clubs; and academic major clubs or organizations.

Category 10 - Admission Prices

This area attempts to discover whether the cost of admission prices or membership dues for certain organizations is a determining factor in establishing or maintaining membership in those organizations.

Category 11 - Activity Locations

This allows students to provide their choice of location for activities to ensure turnout. Options such as dormitories, churches, minority student center buildings, community civic centers, student centers, and academic auditoriums are included here.

Category 12 - Career Development

These questions concern services delivered by the Center for Career Development (or Placement Office) to minority students. Included are Elements dealing with the availability of career information particularly directed at minority students (e.g., material on co-op or job opportunities for minorities), and other related matters.

Category 13 - Academic Advising

Items under this category would deal with academic advising issues. Respondents would be asked to indicate the quality of academic advisement or guidance given by faculty or staff members.

Category 14 - Academic Support Services

This category explores the effectiveness of academic support services such as Learning Assistant Programs (LAP) and similar services.

Category 15 - Counseling Services

The effectiveness of counseling services is the major focus of items in this category. Psychological counseling items are included here.

Category 16 - Open Category

This is an open-ended category in which respondents are encouraged to write down suggestions about areas they feel are important to their success in school which have not been included in the survey.

In developing the instrument, researchers are encouraged to include a section designated as "other" in all items to allow respondents to furnish information not specifically requested.

On the basis of the collected and analyzed data, a number of minority activities can then be implemented. It can not be stressed enough that student involvement is crucial to the success of these programs.

Successful Bradley Programs

From my experience with the minority program at Bradley, I can offer suggestions for implementing effective minority activities.

Minority Student Affairs Advisory Council

This Council consists of a group of minority students who are representatives of all minority organizations such as fraternities, sororities or other organizations. At Bradley University, this group was formed in part as a result of the needs assessment survey conducted in the spring of 1985. It effectively serves as a "clearing house" and is the forum for minority students to air their views and concerns. As the director of this committee, I record their concerns and pass them on to the appropriate university authorities. The advisory council meets every two weeks. This council disseminates information to different minority groups much faster than any other medium.

Minority Student Career Opportunity Task Force

This group is made up of about a dozen minority students representing a variety of constituencies such as the university student senate, Greek organizations, and the Center for Career Development. On the administrative side, we have the Director of Co-curricular Development, the Director of the Office of Career Development and a staff member, the Director of Black Studies, and the Director of Minority Student Services. This task force is charged with the responsibility of organizing the Annual Minority Career Opportunities Buffet and the Minority Job Fair.

Every November we invite professionals from different companies to come and spend three evening hours with our minority students, telling them in a rather informal way what it takes on our students' part to land a job with their companies. Because we invite minority students ranging from freshman through graduate levels, the other facet of this buffet is purely informational. Some of the professionals come to recruit while others come to inform our students of possible career paths. This event is an excellent way to involve our minority community people. We invite local minority attorneys, physicians, nurses, educators, research scientists, community agency workers, college or university professors, and financial professionals, to mention a few.

The task force is also responsible for compiling a minority student resume book. This book is available for $10 to each company or agency which plans to come to our Minority Career Day to recruit. Companies which have attended in the past report that our Minority Career Day allows them to get a very good idea of candidates they might be interested in interviewing.

On Career Day, our minority students meet prospective employers or co-op agencies. This opportunity has been tremendously helpful to our students in their efforts to get jobs. Each year we have more than a hundred representatives from a variety of companies. Depending upon the degree of commitment an institution has in placing its minority students, these two activities can be done on a small or large scale.

Minority Student Recruitment

Twice a year busloads of prospective high school minority students are brought to the Bradley campus for a weekend. Along with receiving information on financial aid and other related issues, these "kids" have an opportunity to hear some of our minority students talk about their experiences at Bradley. The high school kids are paired off with our students and spend the weekend in our students' rooms. They also participate in social or cultural activities organized for that weekend. For a couple of days our students play the role of "mentor," "big brother/sister" if you will. Our students look forward to this activity every year. It helps the prospective students as well as ours.

Minority Student Representative

There is a minority student representative on our University Faculty and Staff Senate Affirmative Action Committee. The student's role is vital because it offers the minority students an opportunity to participate in university politics. This representative actively participates in the discussions and decisions made in this committee. Some of the topics covered include the recruitment of minority students and faculty. At this level the minority student representative has a voting right.

Tutorial Services

A number of minority students find it very difficult to scholastically adjust to the academic demands of an institution such as Bradley University. They find themselves needing tutorial services or similar learning assistance. With this in mind, Bradley University has developed a Learning

Assistance Program (LAP) to help students who need academic tutoring.

Newsletter

One of the needs expressed by many of the minority student respondents who participated in our 1985 needs assessment survey was a newsletter. The need was fulfilled with a monthly newsletter entitled the *NETWORK*, which is mailed to every minority student at Bradley. The newsletter carries the director's editorial and a section for faculty/staff opinions. Minority student organizations can submit information they want announced in the newsletters. The information ranges from activity dates to tutorial opportunities. Our minority students are heavily involved in the production of the newsletter. They type it on the computer, make copies, address the newsletters, and mail them or take them to dormitories and to different drop-off points on campus.

The Personal Touch

As director of minority student services, I have tried to do something that I think is effective. At the end of each semester, after the semester grades are out, I write all minority students who are on scholastic probation a personal letter inviting them to come to my office to discuss their academic problems and to refer them to the appropriate services on campus for assistance. At the same time, I also send personal letters to all minority students who completed the semester with a 3.0 out of a 4.0 grade point average system, congratulating them on a job well done. These two approaches have been highly appreciated by the students.

Summary

This paper has been divided into three major sections by design. The first section was intended to illustrate how complicated it is to define the term "minority." The second section focused on research work related to efforts that have already been made or are being made to provide meaningful programs or activities for minorities on predominantly white campuses. In relating research work included under this section, I was hoping that the handbook users would be able to utilize approaches used by other institutions and also to use the information for further investigation into the issue.

The third and last section dealt with some exemplary programmatic activities which have worked for me and might hopefully be done elsewhere in their entirety or with necessary modifications.

It is my strong feeling that if minority campus activities are to be effective, the directors of minority offices, irrespective of the size or location of their institutions, should start developing programs based upon meaningful research data. Then and only then will they be able to build a reasonably strong case as they solicit financial assistance from university authorities.

References

Appalachia Education Lab. (1988). *Programs of Promise.* A Summary of Current Programs Focusing on the Recruitment of Minority Candidates to Careers in Professional Education. Washington, DC: Educational Research and Improvement.

Calvert, Robert, Jr. (1979). *Affirmative Action: A Comprehensive Recruitment Manual.* Garrett Park, MD: Garrett Park Press.

Cervantes, Oscar F., ed. (1988). *What Universities and Counseling Centers Can Do To Address the Problem of Low Admission, Attrition and Retention of Minority Students.*

Clewell, Beatriz C. (1986). *Improving Minority Retention in Higher Education: A Search for Effective Institutional Practices.* Princeton, NJ: Educational Testing Service.

Garfield, Joan B. & Ramano, John L. (1983). *Retention and Academic Achievement in Higher Education: The General College PEP Program (PEP I, II, III,).* Minneapolis, MN: General College, University of Minnesota.

Kasambira, Paul K. (1986). "Getting minority students to participate." *The Handbook of Minority Student Services.* Charles Taylor (Ed.). Madison, WI: Praxis Publications.

Kelly, Kathleen. (1988). *Mount St. Mary's College, Doheny Campus: A Comprehensive Program of Retention for an Ethnically Diverse Student Body.* Los, Angeles, CA: Mount St. Mary's College, Doheny Campus.

Meha, Arapata T. (1988). *Student Retention: Catalyst for Institutional Change.* Honolulu: Hawaii University-Office of the Chancellor.

Mendoza, Jose. (1988). *Developing and Implementing a Data Base and Microcomputer Tracking System To Track and Serve Minority Students To Enhance Minority Recruitment and Retention.* Arizona: Glendale Community College.

Minority Outreach Task Force. (1988). *Preparing To Win.* Reno: Nevada University System.

Nunez-Wormack, Elsa. (1989). *The National Agenda for Higher Education into the 21st Century.* Keynote address presented at the Statewide Conference on Retention of Minority Students, Ohio State University.

Ramirez, Genevieve M. (1986). *Retention of the Latino University Student: The Case of CSULB.* California.

Smith, Janet D. (1988). *Access, Excellence and Student Retention: The Challenge of Leadership, Public Trust and Institutional Effectiveness in Urban Community Colleges.* Paper presented at the Annual Convention of the Association of Community College Trustees.

Providing Promise: Black Student Leadership on Campus

ABOUT THE AUTHOR:

Lawrence W. Young

Mr. Young has been the Director of the Paul Robeson Cultural Center at Pennsylvania State University since 1982. Lawrence Young attended Miami University in Oxford, Ohio, and earned both a B.S. in Education with major emphasis in English and a masters degree in Education with a concentration in English and Professional Education. In 1969 he was appointed Assistant Director of Black Student Affairs at Miami University, and in subsequent years was appointed Director of Educational Opportunity Programs and Director of Minority Student Affairs at Miami, a position he held until 1982.

Mr. Young has ben involved in a number of organizations, including the NAACP and the National Council for Black Studies. He has had numerous articles published and has been guest editor for NIP magazine and American correspondent for Afromart magazine. He writes on matters which affect the Black community. He has lectured at high schools, colleges, and to professional audiences. He has recently completed a workshop production on alcohol, advertising, and African-Americans. Future plans include completion of doctoral studies, writing a novel, and visiting a free Azania (South Africa).

INTRODUCTION

The National Urban League describes the situation on American campuses regarding minorities as "a crisis and a promise." The crisis is the all-too-common situation of declining minority enrollment and retention, a sometimes openly hostile environment, and in-group bickering within the African-American community. The promise resides with progressive leadership, openmindedness, and the strength to take action to make students feel comfortable and wanted.

Significant policy changes must occur as a matter of course, not merely in reaction to extreme situations or in order to garner political academic notice. Colleges which fail to take positive action will find themselves in de facto support of the status quo, again isolated from real social intercourse. Perhaps of more immediate nonacademic interest, they will also find themselves facing dwindling minority enrollment as those students take themselves, and their dollars, to schools which show a good record of recruiting, retaining, and graduating minorities.

This paper will examine ways in which staff and personnel can help make their campus a place where minority students are welcomed and successful. The focus will be on how the minority affairs staff is crucial -- in acting as role models, networking, mentoring, assessing and impacting the campus climate, and developing black student leadership.

PROVIDING PROMISE:

**Black Student
Leadership
On Campus**

by
**Lawrence W.
Young**

The news on college campuses across the country about Black students is bleak. Numbers are dropping to lows not seen since the early sixties. Those students who are enrolled are finding themselves under siege by neo-racists who resent their presence. Further exacerbating the tenuous position of Black students on campus is the existence of sporadic internecine warfare and enmity between Black males and females and among Black males. Each of these conditions alone could contribute to a high attrition rate for Black students and in combination they create a situation which borders on disaster. When we note the relatively low number of Black faculty and staff members and further note that there is an underrepresentation of Black males at every level of the higher education pyramid, there appears to be little reason for optimism.

Yet the National Urban League, in its volume *The State Of Black America 1989*, states that we face a "crisis and a promise." The promise lies within individual institutions which, under the progressive leadership of forward thinking administrators, have undertaken positive remedies for some of these ills. Additionally, those universities which are lagging in their attention to these situations have been sobered by the report, *One-Third Of A Nation*, published by the American Council on Education and the Education Commission of the States. This report notes that universities that fail to initiate policy changes to meet the needs of a changing populace not only harm that populace, but also harm themselves and the society in general.

The purpose of this paper is to examine the role that minority affairs staff, and student services personnel in general, can and must play in the diminution of these problems and how these staff persons can be on the cutting edge of the provision of leadership in creating the new academy that meets the challenges that a changing population and the advent of the twenty-first century will bring.

I will focus on how minority affairs staff will be crucial in the areas of role modeling, developing networks, serving as mentors to younger professionals, assessing and impacting the campus climate for minorities, and broadening the role of minority affairs officers as teachers.

> Leadership and learning are indispensable to each other.
> -John F. Kennedy

There is a continuing tendency in academia to equate leadership with titles. There is the assumption by many that the "universal Ph.D." endows one with reasonable solutions to all problems. I and several of my college classmates were disabused of that belief early in our college careers when we were referred to the one Black faculty member on campus for some assistance in adjusting to an overwhelmingly white environment. His advice was "just don't think about it." When we turned with the same concerns to the one Black janitor on campus, we had an entirely new world opened up to us. He referred us to books about Blacks, related to us the coping mechanisms others before us had used, and supplied us with information about how to access the slender yet substantial social support system available in a rural setting. To be sure, some of us were still unable to cope, yet a surprising number of us, using this underground leadership and learning system, survived and thrived.

From my perspective it is essential that anyone who would be in a position to provide leadership to Black students must also be able and willing to teach those students as well. And if one is to be a leader/teacher, the questions of "leading to where?" and "teaching what?" will have to be addressed. Many Black students come to view a college education as an end unto itself, a means by which to gain access to personal prestige, privilege, and prosperity. Others are confused about the value of an education and may even feel guilty about attending college. Yet another group may have a dimly defined nationalistic philosophy through which they somehow see themselves devoting their education and their future work to "the needs of the masses." Each of these groups is in need of teaching and leadership and each will represent a unique challenge.

It should be clear to the student services practitioner that attempting to provide leadership and learning is fraught with danger, particularly if we consider the anxieties, skepticism, and paranoia that pervades the Black community. On many campuses Black faculty and staff who were motivated by commitment and love of Black people have been castigated as sell-outs for critically analyzing another's strategy, for breaking "group solidarity" on some issue. Leadership and teaching involves honor, integrity, vision and values. For whatever reasons, those principles appear to be in short supply within the larger society and selfishness, greed, deceit, and pragmatism seem to be in control. The question we must face is whether we will allow the succeeding generation to continue down a path that has been so clearly destructive to society. Because national leaders do not appear to have learned anything from the last ten years, must campus leaders follow their abysmal example?

Black leadership must be about more than position and prestige. Black leadership on a college campus evolves from commitment, study, understanding, and the possession of a functional value system which clearly recognizes the reality of Black people. Black leadership on a college campus includes the ability to develop the love that Martin Luther King, Jr. called *Agape*, or love of one's neighbor. This would mean that those who would provide leadership for Black students (or other minority/underrepresented groups) would, of necessity, have to have a strong empathetic feeling for those students that could be defined as "love." That love would move one to act in the best interests of those students at all times and not allow frustrations to deter one from certain objectives.

A necessary task for that empathetic leader would also be to teach those with whom he or she works to love and respect themselves and others like themselves. The negative self-concept of minorities, reinforced regularly by politicians and the media, can only be offset by a concerted, systematic and continuing program of positive reinforcement. For every Willie Horton presented there must be a dozen Reginald Lewis's and Barbara Proctors presented. As a leader, the minority affairs coordinator must be able to teach about the culture and the contributions to society of the targeted group. And because culture is a dynamic, ever changing phenomenon, the leader must be willing to upgrade his or her knowledge on a regular basis and in essence become an eternal student as well as teacher.

John W. Gardner, in his book *Morale*, states:

> There is risk for those who take the lead in rebuilding. People who act and initiate make mistakes. People seeking the path to the future often wind up in blind alleys. Those who have the confidence to act creatively to regenerate the society must also have the humility to know the danger of overestimating what they can accomplish.

Poet Haki Madhubiti calls for Black leaders to be "visionary" and "motivated activists." A leader must be moved by certain values and beliefs and want the very best of life for those he or she would lead. Those who would lead should remember that:

> Where there is no vision, the people perish.
> Prov. 29:18

Imparting Values

There is a great deal of debate on whether the role of the academy should include the imparting of values. This debate tends to assume that values have not been and are not now an integral part of the educational process in America. Americans of African descent have over the years and with few exceptions bought into the mainstream value system with its emphasis on individualism, capitalism, imperialism, and racism. No matter that these values pit Black Americans against themselves and

their victimized counterparts around the world. The educational process within the academy actively reinforces these values and is constantly on guard to any challenge to the validity and primacy of these values. While the debates at Stanford University in 1988 were ostensibly over a body of literature and the need for that body to be inclusive, the real battle was over whose values would be presented to students in the future and whether the values of the "canon" should be allowed to be challenged.

As teachers and leaders, the minority affairs and student personnel staff members who have internalized positive feelings of empathy with their charges will see significant parts of their role to be a challenger of some values, a reinforcer of other values, and a teacher of some values. The question to be answered is, which values shall be imparted?

If the practitioner is aware of the scholarship and the writings of people like Dr. Frances Cress-Welsing, Sonia Sanchez, Haki Madhubuti, Gwendolyn Brooks, Na'im Akbar, Molefi Asante, and Maulana Karenga, among a host of others, then a value system based on the needs and the experience of African-Americans becomes evident. Of course reading the daily newspaper of any metropolitan area or the National Urban League's *Annual State of Black America* report will also make it clear that something is not working right for the majority of Black Americans. It must be contended that many dysfunctional behaviors which result in truncated life opportunities and premature death are a measure and result of the values attached to those lives.

When he formulated the "Nguzo Saba" (Seven Principles) in 1965, Maulana Karenga was responding to what was viewed as the key crisis in Black life. He characterized this crisis as:

> ...the critical lack of a coherent system of views and values that would give them a moral, material and meaningful interpretation of life as well as demand an allegiance and practice which would insure their liberation and a higher level of human life.

Thus Karenga concluded that a functional set of values should be presented to the Black community through which they might begin to see themselves differently and to redefine and reshape reality in their own image. The Nguzo Saba as a part of the Kwanzaa celebration serves as a framework of values that will provide a foundation for young and old alike. It is essential that the young college age Black student be provided with some exposure to these principles, for they speak to both the problems and the solutions that confront Black America.

Those principles (values) are:

1. **UMOJA** (Unity)
   for family, community, nation, and race.

2. **KUJICHAGULIA** (Self-determination)
   to define ourselves, name ourselves, create for ourselves, and speak for ourselves.

3. **UJIMA** (Collective work and responsibilty)
   to build and maintain our community together and solve problems together.

4. **UJAMAA** (Collective economics)
   to build and maintain businesses and profit from them together.

5. **NIA** (Purpose)
   to make a collective vocation of developing our community.

6. **KUUMBA** (Creativity)
   to work to beautify the community

7. **IMANI** (Faith)
   to believe in our people, parents, teachers, and leaders.

A leader who tries to live by these values, who incorporates them, where possible, into her or his work, and who attempts to impart these values to young people is doing a tremendous service to the community and to the psyche of Black students. Stressing these values may reduce the kind of intergroup friction and stress which can hasten the attrition rate. Moreover, these values have an underlying emphasis on respect for self and for others. Every opportunity to reinforce the concept of mutual respect must be seized, since many of the outbreaks of intergroup warfare stem from a lack of respect for a person or a group and generally that lack of respect has a flimsy foundation.

Groups and Individuals

Conventional wisdom tends to lump Black students into a kind of monolithic, homogeneous grouping, where each member has the same background, the same needs, and the same aspirations. While this may be an easy and convenient way to view Black students, it is also an erroneous and simplistic way to view them. The spectrum of Black students extends from the poor to the wealthy, from the marginal to the exceptional, from the politically naive to the politically hyperactive, from the socially unconscious to the radically conscious, from Democrat to Republican to Socialist, and on and on.

Anyone who attempts to deal with this melange as some sort of undifferentiated unit is certain to meet with frustration if not disaster. Yet on most predominantly white campuses there is at least a veneer of unity among the Black students and in some cases there is even the appearance of being a large extended family. Inevitably, group and individual conflicts will arise and cause dissension. Yet the presence and the threat of racist attack and reaction on individuals or groups supplies just enough glue to maintain a minimal level of unity.

The staff person involved in a leadership role with Black students may have to juggle a great deal of information and adopt approaches to suit the stage of awareness and the needs of the individual. Some sensitivity to the tensions under which Black students co-exist with their peers is also necessary. The leader who is viewed as partial to a particular group or point of view is lost to those who have a differing point of view. The most vivid example of this is when students who consider any student who socializes with white students as a traitor to group solidarity. Those who were once termed "oreos" are now termed "blights" or black/whites. This pejorative terminology further alienates the recipient and hardens the belief that "militant Blacks" want to be separated from whites.

The leader's role in this is to somehow be the bridge that brings those two divergent views closer together. Black students need to be made to understand that coalition building is a fine and necessary art and that building functional and beneficial coalitions in no way compromises the integrity of one's blackness.

An interesting, if sometimes disquieting phenomenon, is the burgeoning number of Black student interest and social groups which seem to be appearing on campus. From the Black Greek -letter organizations and Black Student Unions and organizations of the sixties and seventies, we now see specialized organizations for Black journalists, accountants, engineers, architects, medical students, pre-law, and other discipline based areas, as well as organizations for Black women, Black music, and non-Greek social groupings. Although several researchers (Sedlacek and Brooks, 1978) have pointed out the value of retention of Black students, the very proliferation of groups and organizations may hinder the student services practitioner by creating greater competition for too few resources and by developing counterproductive attitudes and behaviors, sometimes motivated by jealousy, between the groups. The leader must be aware of these tensions, try to work with all of the groups and where possible act to coordinate the activities of these groups in a mutually beneficial manner. This is a complex undertaking and it is full of pitfalls, yet unless it is pursued, chaos may reign.

While intra-group conflicts may take up a great deal of time and energy, the student services personnel who work with Black and other minority group students must be constantly alert to the potential for inter-group conflict which has the potential to boil over into physical conflict as it did on several campuses in the last several years. Of particular concern recently has been the volatile issue of who should be invited to campus to speak. Black students feel justified in protesting speeches by Klan members, reactionary politicians and others whose record of racist antipathy or antagonism have been established.

On the other hand, Black students can expect and should anticipate a strong negative reaction from Jewish organizations and others when invitations are extended to Minister Louis Farrakhan or other members of the Nation of Islam, who have, rightly or wrongly, been accused of anti-Semitism. This same reaction has been experienced by Black students who have invited certain "Rap" groups and other political personalities to campus. While the values of freedom of speech and the right to protest are understood and accepted, it is incumbent upon both Black and white leadership on the campus to channel the feelings of anger and hostility and create a learning experience for all parties. Through creative planning and cooperative execution, leaders may use these confrontations for both learning and teaching about the anxieties, the fears and the pain of disparate groups.

Minority affairs and student services personnel may wish to give some specific attention to the conflict on campus that may arise between Black athletes and other Black students. While this may be viewed as an intragroup conflict, very often the nature of the athletic experience, the demands, the special treatment, and expectations, makes the Black athlete on campus a group apart. Sadly we would note that on some campuses the largest group of Black students fall into the athlete category. Conflicts arise over requests for special privileges, perceived indifference to the problems of racism by athletes and competition for dates. Communications between coaches, minority affairs and student services staff, and all of the students, is an essential ingredient to the resolution of this type of conflict. The minority affairs staff person has a delicate role in that he or she must walk the tightrope between the two groups without being perceived as being for or against one or the other. Inevitably the minority affairs officer will face conflict situations which will test her or his values and beliefs and may place that officer in a no-win position. Anyone who enters this professional pursuit should be prepared to encounter contradictions and unsatisfactory resolutions.

Impacting Campus Climate

As has been previously stated and well-documented through a number of unpleasant incidents, the climate on campus at some white universities for African-American students can be quite cool. Students are placed in a position of having not only to study and learn, but also to cope with hostility and indifference, be anxious about their physical safety, be the subject of scrutiny and observation by the insensitive, and create a social and cultural life for themselves that they find comfortable and rewarding.

Those in positions of leadership who are expected to work with minority students have an obligation to assist in the provision of a healthy and safe environment in which young people may grow. Ideally, this should be part of the role of every staff person, every faculty member, every administrator and every student. Realistically, much (often too much) of that burden is placed on the shoulders of the minority affairs officer when Black students are concerned.

To be effective in changing the campus climate for Black and other minority students, the leader must enlist the assistance of an array of campus officers and resources. There must be the insistence of some clearly stated and unambiguous university-wide policy to deal with acts of racial intimidation,

violence, and intolerance. This policy should include some form of university sanction against verbal and written slurs, since this is one of the most frequently employed methods of attack used by the mean-spirited. It is recognized and accepted that First Amendment rights disallows sanctions against speech; however, the leader can and should argue that the courts have pointed out that certain forms of speech can be sanctioned. Moreover, it is time for all of those in higher education to understand the fact that in some instances a word can inflict more damage to the individual than rocks, clubs or bullets. If a university will not permit someone to be brutalized physically, what rationale allows that same university to stand by idly while some of its students are brutalized verbally? The minority affairs staff person should be vigorous on this issue since nothing, short of physical violence, so destroys the climate as the existence of poisoned tongues. Through interaction with the conduct standards officer or the disciplinary board, the minority affairs officer can make a case for certain sanctions in cases involving racially abusive speech.

Because some Black students have a well founded fear of physical violence, the minority affairs staff persons should consider means and methods to provide the best possible physical safety arrangements for Black students. This may mean collaborating with the campus safety director to learn about escort services or to establish routes of patrol by safety officers for late night events attended by Black students. Here again the minority affairs officer must walk a fine line. Some Black students insist on having social events that begin at midnight or later and want to use university facilities for such events. Those personnel who deny these requests are regarded as "not working in the best interests of Black students." While we may understand the inability of young people to see all of the academic implications of a Saturday night event that starts at midnight and ends at 5am, the stance of those in leadership positions has to be to advance the academic mission above any other considerations, particularly social ones. Students have to be encouraged and persuaded to recognize that while a well-rounded social life is a part of the campus experience, some social events,by their very nature, detract from, rather than contribute to the goals and objectives of students and their parents. Because this age group is generally trusting and naive and feel themselves to be invulnerable, they often take tragic risks to their person and their academic welfare. The minority affairs leader/ teacher must be active in adding balance between the social desires and the academic needs of minority students, as well as assisting students in making wise and healthy choices.

The role of the minority affairs officer as teacher of majority group members is often ignored or viewed as invalid. Yet there is ample documentation that much of the racial antagonism and animosity is based upon ignorance, false information and assumptions, sometimes fed by cynical leaders and sensation-seeking media. An example of this is the commonly held mythology in the majority community of the "Black male rapist." Recent studies have shown that the vast majority of rapes are perpetrated by acquaintances of the victim, particularly on campus. The minority affairs leader should be actively involved in workshops, staff meetings and other venues in which she or he may impact on the false beliefs and negative attitudes of majority group members which may harm the students. This would have to include as many opportunities to interact with majority students as possible, since those students have the potential to make the environment repugnant or constructive.

> It is time for a new generation of leadership to cope with new problems and new opportunities, for there is a new world to be won.
>
> -John F. Kennedy

The academy has begun to face the reality of a changing population and all that entails. The reality of racial and cultural diversity within the student body of tomorrow means that the academy must begin preparing for those students today. This means greater pressure and demands will be placed on those assigned to work with the minority population.

As the population of minority students grows, so will demands on the resources of the minority affairs officer. That person will rightfully be asked to serve as a role model for all students and as such he or she must exhibit the highest levels of integrity and character. As a campus leader who has vision, the minority affairs officer must have the courage to challenge the status quo and the creativity to offer new and acceptable ideas for educating young people. As a campus leader, the minority affairs officer must be willing to extend her or his network of allies to include all of those who can and should provide the necessary services and goods that make the collegiate living experience a valuable and rewarding one. In some cases this will include an outreach into the surrounding and supporting community, which may also need to understand that some changes in behaviors will be beneficial to them as well as to the university. The minority affairs officer's network among students will have to be extensive, both for the reception and the dissemination of vital information.

The keys to establishing and maintaining effective networks are reliability and trust. An unreliable leader is no leader at all, and when the minority affairs officer loses the trust of the majority of African-American students and staff, then that person will become so ineffective as to be a liability to the academy.

The minority affairs officer has one task that is so vitally important that the failure to carry it through jeopardizes any other things which may be accomplished. A leader must guarantee that if she or he is no longer in place, the mission, the values and the objectives will go forward. To insure that in some future time when personnel change, when the academy refocuses its mission, or when societal pressures subside, that the hard-won gains of yesterday do not become footnotes in the university's history, the minority affairs officer must serve as a mentor to those who will be trained to follow. Without a next generation of courageous and committed young leaders willing to forgo the opportunity for mega-buck salaries in the corporate sector and stake their claim as the heirs to the progress made by the seniors, lifetimes of work may be wasted and washed away. Service as a mentor to a young, conscious, and committed educator may be the only guarantee that minority affairs officers may have that their efforts will be sustained, carried further and institutionalized in such a way as to become a permanent part of the life of the academy. If we believe that the work that we do is valuable and worthwhile then we must be about the business of replicating our vision and our zeal for what we do in the imaginations of others.

Leader, teacher, mentor: these roles are a necessary and vital part of the educational process. Black and minority students must be served by competent professionals who understand that the challenge of education in the 21st century will be the challenge of justice as well as the challenge of the survivability of our society. As ironic as it may sound, the destiny of America will lie in the hands of America's minority populations, so lately despised and disparaged. We have always known that our fate was inextricable from that of the society at large. This new reality must be taught and learned quickly. Those who would wear the mantle of leadership have an enormous responsibility and obligation in the reshaping of society. The challenge has been issued. Who will answer?

References

American Council on Education and the Education Commission of the States. (1988). *One Third Of A Nation. A Report of the Commission on Minority Participation in Education and American Life.*

Gardner, John W. (1978). *Morale.* New York: W.W. Norton & Co. Inc.

Karenga, Maulana. (1977). *Kwanzaa: Origin, Concepts, Practices.* Los Angeles: Kawaida Publications.

Sedlacek, William E. & Brooks, Glenwood C. (1978). *Racism In American Education: A Model for Change.* Chicago: Nelson-Hall.

MINORITY STUDENT DIRECTORY:

Create a sense of community on campus

by
Dr. Charles
Taylor

A directory is another tool that you can use to improve minority student retention rates. Ideally, it should be compiled before the fall semester starts and distributed during a special orientation. The faster students have access to it, the sooner they will be able to benefit from it.

You can use the student survey on page 39 to compile data for the directory. A sample directory entry is located at the end of the survey. By working with the registrar, admissions, minority services and other students service offices, you should be able to obtain the names and addresses of all new and continuing minority students. The survey can be mailed to students during the summer. Plan to do additional mail and phone follow-up after your initial mailing has gone out, as this will increase your response rate. If your response rate is still unsatisfactory after you follow-up, you may want to wait until students are back on campus to complete your survey and concentrate on those students who have not completed the survey.

To ensure a "filled" directory, you may want to set up a two or three day "telemarketing" room where you have either volunteers or workstudy students call students and actually fill out the forms over the phone. However, you will need to write a telephone script to improve your chances of getting accurate information on all the questions.

Since, for the most part, the information included in the directory is "public" information, issues of confidentiality are not a problem. However, to prepare for such questions, consult with your campus legal advisor on ways to ensure confidentiality. Find out how this issue is handled when the traditional student campus directory is compiled. By using a computer data base program, the information gathered can be sorted and categorized as appropriate.

You should give some thought to how you plan

to arrange your directory. The goal should be to make the directory "user friendly," so that students will use it throughout the year. Your table of contents should be comprehensive. Student entries in the directory can be organized by race. For example, you can have a chapter that includes survey information on African, Asian, Hispanic, and Native Americans. Within the racial categories, you can further divide entries by sex. This makes it easy for students to locate peers of the same sex for studying, exercising, etc. The directory can further be categorized by class standing, facilitating in-class interaction. Other categories you might consider are in-state, out-of-state, and majors. The data base program you use will make this a relatively painless task.

You can stop with this very basic directory, or you can add a few more pages to make the directory even more useful. A section can be added on campus and community resources. In the campus section, you could list minority student organizations, fraternities and sororities, various student services offices on campus, deadlines and contacts of key faculty, administrators and students. Under the community resource sections, you might list minority-owned beauty and barber shops, businesses and nightclubs, churches, minority community-based organizations, and information on "What to do in town."

The directory does not have to be large or costly. If carefully thought-out, it can be compiled inexpensively. If you get a student graphic artist to design and layout the cover, and use desktop publishing software, you can end up with a very professional, attractive directory that could become the students' "bible." Using your school's mascot or logo on the cover strengthens students' identification with the school.

If your budget simply cannot support an additional expenditure, try to get local businesses or minority organizations to sponsor the directory. Coupons and /or other advertising can be put in the back of the directory so the sponsor gets acknowledged.

After the directory is returned from the printer, call a meeting and invite all students who are listed in the directory. Ideally, this would be 90% of students of color on your campus.

After passing out the directory, walk students through the table of contents. Explain to them the purpose of the directory. Suggest ways they can use the directory (e.g., find tutors, study partners, etc.). Tell them not to misuse the directory or infringe upon someone's expertise if that person is not interested in their solicitations. Encourage a dialogue about the directory. This dialogue is helpful in providing parameters on how students feel it should be used. The dialogue tends to get students excited about the possibilities. It also makes them aware of the skills they and their peers possess, and this usually has a positive impact because it stresses self-help, which can be empowering.

Some campuses have experienced success with same-sex meetings, where females or males can meet each other in a supportive, non-threatening environment. Consider such a meeting on your campus as well. This meeting if used wisely can build a sense of community among students where they view each other as colleagues instead of competitors.

Make copies of the *Minority Student Directory* available to student services staff. You may be pleasantly surprised at the creative uses such staff will make of the directory. You may also want to make copies available to the faculty and other campus administrators, depending on your budget and the numbers involved. Just be sure to send a cover letter when you distribute the directory so that everyone is aware of its purpose. You may find the *Minority Student Directory* becoming a "must have" on your campus.

STUDENT SURVEY

Instructions

(Name of your program) is interested in improving the quality of services delivered to students of color. Your response to this survey will assist our office in planning programs and activities that reflect your interests and enhance your academic career. We are also compiling a directory that will include information about you and your fellow students to encourage networking. Please answer each item below. Remember to sign the statement at the end of the survey to be included in the Student Directory. Only information starred(*) will be included in the directory.

Demographics

*1. Name_____

*2. SS#_____

*3. Home Address_____

*4. Campus Address_____

*5. Home Telephone_____

*6. Campus Telephone_____

*7. Ethnic Group (check one)
   ☐ Asian American
   ☐ African American
   ☐ Hispanic American
   ☐ Native American
   ☐ White American
   ☐ Other (fill in)_____

*8. Sex
   ☐ Female   ☐ Male

*9. Year in School
   ☐ Fr ☐ So ☐ Jr ☐ Sr
   ☐ Other_____

Skill-Bank

*10. I possess (check all that apply):

__ Newsletter experience
__ Student government experience
__ Photography experience
__ Media experience (list type)_____
__ Research experience
__ Artistic ability
__ Computer skills
(describe software you're familiar with)

_____
_____

__ Other (describe)

_____
_____
_____

Interests

*11. Check level of interest in each item

Item	Interest		
	High	Some	Little
Leadership training	__	__	__
Making new friends	__	__	__
Working on a newsletter	__	__	__
Joining a Fraternity/Sorority	__	__	__
Cross-cultural activities	__	__	__
Student government	__	__	__
Serving on a committee	__	__	__
Community Service	__	__	__
Working with computers	__	__	__
Forming study groups	__	__	__
Mentor relationships	__	__	__
Social activities	__	__	__
Other (fill in)_____	__	__	__

Staying Informed

12. What is the likelihood that each of the following would be effective in keeping you informed of campus activities?

Method	Likelihood		
	High	Med	Low
Campus Newspaper	__	__	__
Bulletin Boards	__	__	__
Campus TV	__	__	__
Student Organization	__	__	__
Newsletter	__	__	__
Posters	__	__	__
Mailbox flyers	__	__	__
Word-of-mouth	__	__	__
Other (fill in)_____	__	__	__

_____

Social Activities

*13. Which of the following social activies would you attend? (check all that apply)

__ Plays
__ Sports events
__ Movies
__ Outdoor activities
__ Dances
__ Lectures/Speakers
__ Nightclub events
__ Art exhibits
__ Concerts

*Which of the following types of movies would you attend? (check all that apply)

__ Horror
__ Mystery
__ Comedy
__ Documentaries
__ Science fiction
__ Musical
__ Other _____

*14. Number your top three music choices:

__ Soul   __ Reggae   __ Rap
__ Jazz   __ Gospel   __ Blues
__ Rock   __ Country
__ Other _____

*15. Number your top three speaker choices:

__ Minority issues   __ Civil rights issues
__ Political issues   __ Educational issues
__ Women's issues   __ Comedy
__ Other(s)_____

*16. What is your major? _____

*17. In which course would you like to have tutors or study groups? List as many courses as appropriate.

__ History   __ Business   __ Math
__ Science   __ Foreign Language
__ English   __ Computer Science
__ Other(s) _____

*18. I am able to tutor the following areas. Fill in only if you made a B or better in the course. List as many courses as appropriate. (If you are unable to tutor, skip to next question.)

__ History   __ Business   __ Math
__ Science   __ Foreign Language
__ English   __ Computer Science
__ Other(s) _____

19. You have my permission to include the items starred with asterisks above in the Student Directory. It is my understanding that this directory will be distributed to students of color to help us find tutors, form new friendships, and network with each other.

Date _____
Student Signature _____

20. (Fill in below only if you don't want all items mentioned above included in this directory.)

__ It's okay to include me in the Student Directory, but please leave out items(s) number(ed): _____

Thank you for completing this survey. Your response will assist us in bringing better services to students on campus. Please return this survey to:

(Put return address here)

An example of a typical directory entry:

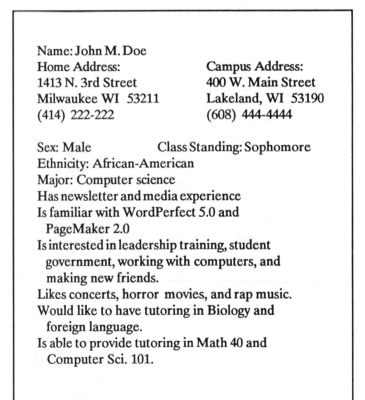

Name: John M. Doe
Home Address: Campus Address:
1413 N. 3rd Street   400 W. Main Street
Milwaukee WI 53211   Lakeland, WI 53190
(414) 222-222   (608) 444-4444

Sex: Male   Class Standing: Sophomore
Ethnicity: African-American
Major: Computer science
Has newsletter and media experience
Is familiar with WordPerfect 5.0 and
   PageMaker 2.0
Is interested in leadership training, student
   government, working with computers, and
   making new friends.
Likes concerts, horror movies, and rap music.
Would like to have tutoring in Biology and
   foreign language.
Is able to provide tutoring in Math 40 and
   Computer Sci. 101.

STUDENT EVALUATION OF MINORITY STUDENT DIRECTORY

Instructions

Please answer all items on this questionnaire. We are interested in your perceptions of the effectiveness of the Minority Student Directory you were listed in this academic year. Your evaluation will help us in rendering better service to future participants. There are no right or wrong answers. You will not be identified in any way. Please do not include your name on this evaluation. When you have finished, return the evaluation in the enclosed addressed envelope.

1. Sex ____Female ____Male

2. Year in School

___FR ___SO ___JR ___SR ___Other_____

3. Ethnic Group

___Asian
___White
___Black
___Hispanic
___Native American
___Other_____

4. Do you feel there is a positive or negative feeling associated with being listed in the Directory?

___Positive ___Negative ___Both

___Describe the feeling_____

_____

_____

5. Do you think the directory should be continued?

___Yes ___No ___Not Sure

Explain_____

_____

_____

6. How did you use the directory (check all that apply)

___To find a tutor   ___To obtain dates
___To meet new friends ___To network
___Other_____

7. Did your listing in the directory cause you to experience any of the things described below?

		Yes	No
a.	New friendships	___	___
b.	Determination to graduate	___	___
c.	New study partners	___	___
d.	More confident about myself	___	___
e.	Feelings of belonging on campus	___	___
f.	More opportunities on campus	___	___
g.	Increased motivation to study	___	___
h.	More peers contacting you	___	___
i.	More contact by staff and faculty	___	___
j.	More tutoring opportunities	___	___
k.	Invitations to more social activities	___	___
l.	Other _____		

_____

8. How would you describe your overall reaction to the directory? Circle one

   a. Extremely effective
   b. Very effective
   c. Effective
   d. Not effective
   e. Extremely ineffective
Explain _____

9. How often did you make use of the directory? Circle one

   a. Daily   b. Weekly
   c. Twice a week d. Monthly
   e. Very seldom f. Never

10. How can the directory be improved?

_____

_____

    Thank you for completing this evaluation. Please place this evaluation in the enclosed envelope provided and drop it in the mail.

The Role of Faculty in the Retention of Minority Students

ABOUT THE AUTHOR:

Dr. C. Scully
Stikes

Dr. Stikes is the Dean of the division of Liberal Arts and Sciences at Milwaukee Area Technical College. Immediately prior to this, he was Assistant Chancellor for Student Affairs at the University of Wisconsin-Milwaukee. He is also the sole proprietor of Development Services, International, an educational and management consulting firm that he has operated since 1969.

Dr. Stikes attended Kent State University on an athletic scholarship, and there he received his B.A. in Psychology and Biological Sciences (1967), M.Ed. in Rehabilitation Counseling (1969), M.A. in Sociology and Anthropology (1970), and Ph.D. in Counseling and Organizational Development with a minor in Sociology and Anthropology (1974).

Dr. Stikes has published many articles about cultural variables in education and counseling, and is an active lecturer and workshop participant, having had more than 400 speaking engagements. His speeches have spanned a wide field, addressing topics from counseling and human potential to Black and world history.

INTRODUCTION

Two of the most important factors influencing student retention are grades and student involvement. If ways can be found to involve students more in the environment and life of the institution, then the chances of their staying in college are improved. Increased contact and involvement with the faculty can address both of these factors.

Effective faculty involvement requires understanding. To achieve this, it may be helpful for faculty to use a model such as The Authentic Behavioral System Model presented in this article. This model of human interaction and development is offered as a backdrop against which to consider issues and variables in retention of minority students. The model is presented along with six questions that must be asked and answered from both the counselor's (faculty) point of view and the student's. Before a course of action can be decided, the necessity for and consequence of change must be examined. There are six other questions offered which are meant to help determine these consequences, and the author provides an application of the model to a case study.

Specific recommendations for faculty action are provided as well as an example of an authentic and appropriate way to approach teaching mathematics to under-prepared minority students.

THE ROLE OF FACULTY

In the Retention of Minority Students

by
Dr. C. Scully Stikes

Important Issues in Retention

Minority students tend to drop out at higher rates than majority students because they do not perceive that their needs are being met. They are generally more dissatisfied with services, the environment, relationships, and the curriculum (Stikes, 1982). It is clear that facilitating retention of minority students is a complex task. It is complex because there are so many interacting variables including:

-the culture and ethnicity of students;
-socioeconomic background;
-family background;
-gender;
-personal attributes, skills and abilities;
-the developmental stage in which the students encounter higher education, (adolescence, young adulthood or mature adulthood);
-certain personality development factors;
-the institutional culture of a particular college or university campus;
-the personal coping strategies of students and personal relationships;
-the formal institutional strategies to educate the students and the informal community activities in which the students are engaged;
-the students' personal sense of power and locus of control, self-confidence, self esteem;
-the social forces or powers exerted by the society affecting the institution and the institutional power to change;
-the individual goals set by the students themselves and patterns to achieve those goals,
-as well as the institutional goals and strategies related to minority students' development or the lack thereof;
-the personal meanings, ideals, values and commitments students make toward their goals;
-and the institutional values, ideals, and commitments to aid the students in their quest for an education (Stikes, 1989).

The task here is to identify those areas in which the faculty can exert influence and/or control in order to make a difference in the lives of the students. Attrition is a complex result of all the above variables. Any attempt to isolate one cause or factor is a misguided approach to the issues.

In working with any student, the student's fit with the environment, his or her self-management skills, and particular institutional policies and practices are key issues. Institutional offices must eliminate isolation and strive for involvement; they must eliminate the discrepancy between what is expected and what is experienced; and finally, they must facilitate the development of the skill and abilities to acquire good grades. Campus offices must balance between managing the institution to ensure student development while achieving educational excellence (Astin, 1985; Astin 1987; Tinto, 1987) and remain sensitive to issues of class, residence status, age, gender, and racial/ethnic composition (ACT, 1979; Astin, 1977; Stikes, 1984).

The combination of personal characteristics that increases the chances of success of individual minority students include:

-positive self-concept development or self-confidence;
-realistic self-appraisal of strengths and weaknesses;
-the understanding of racism;
-leadership activities;
-community involvement or service;
acquired knowledge or skill in an area;
-a strong support person to turn to who may be on or off campus; and
-willingness to plan ahead to meet long-range goals (Sedlacek and Brooks, 1979).

Armed with knowledge, faculty can be aware of personal attrition factors that affect students' propensity to drop out, and this could help in orienting students to campus and planning their university lives. How students are advised is important. Advising students of their prospects for persisting, academic options, opportunities to upgrade skills, and options in financial aid, housing, and extracurricular activities will affect dropout rates. Further, advisors should remember that there should be caution exercised in advising students to take a leave of absence. A large number of students who do this fail to return. The educational value of stopping-out or dropping-out has not been clearly established for large groups of students (Astin, 1977).

Two key factors in enhancing retention seem to be getting students to spend more time on campus and getting them involved both academically and extracurricularly. In order to achieve academic and social involvement, the institution has to involve the faculty, student services, and academic divisions in policy development, implementation, monitoring, and evaluation. This is a difficult task; however, it is one that can be done with clear goals and flexibility. Each segment of a college/university must contribute to the persistence, retention, and graduation of minority students (Stikes,1984). The issue of student empowerment is important; special activities recognizing the complexity of students lives in the college/university environment should be organized in such a way as to both inform and involve students.

Environmental circumstances play a role in affecting retention that faculty should be aware of:

Students from urban environments persist better in larger institutions (20,000 plus) than students from farms or small towns, and the latter do better at smaller schools.

Students who live on campus seem to persist better than those who do not.

Women living away from home or off campus do not persist as well as those at home.

Those students who work at jobs off campus full-time do not persist as well as those who work on campus nor do they persist as well as those who work part-time (Astin, 1977).

Furthermore, the urban commuter campus has some unique problems regarding retention. The student population is generally older; most students have additional responsibilities such as full-time jobs and families. They may be dividing their time between these important activities and attending school. Since there are generally few housing facilities on commuter campuses, attrition is higher at these institutions. Also, many of these students attend part-time and may attend in the evening. Thses students are more likely to drop out of school, or take longer than the traditional four years to graduate. At four-year commuter colleges, only about 10 to 15 percent of the students attending graduate in four years (Avakian, MacKinney and Allen, 1982).

A critical factor in selecting and attending a particular school and remaining there is financial aid. The kind of financial aid available is as important as the amount. Loans should be avoided, if possible; this is particularly true for men. Loans tend to decrease persistence and to create financial problems later on. Grants are associated with small increases in persistence (Astin, 1977).

A Conceptual System for Retention in College

To enable faculty to address these complex issues, there has to be a comprehensive conceptualization of the process of encouraging persistence and retention in institutions. A model that serves as a mechanism for understanding the student, diagnosing the problem(s)he or she is having, and prescribing change is needed. *The Authentic Behavioral System Model* is one that fulfills these criteria. Diagram One, page 57, illustrates the model and shows the interrelated variables.

Authenticity in the model refers to the activities, relationships, structures, etc. whose underlying processes are responsive to comprehensive human needs with regard for the diversity of human existence. Authenticity requires that a person be conscious, committed, and participate in sharing personal, institutional, and societal power. Too many higher education institutions are inauthentic for persons of color. "A relationship, institution, or society is inauthentic if it gives the appearance of responsiveness while the underlying condition is alienating" (Etzioni, 1968). Inauthentic institutions seem to invest a lot in manipulative activities (Etzioni, 1968). The person who is aware of inauthentic conditions feels manipulated and there is a sense that one shares in one's own manipulation. This allows gestures and facades to substitute for real change and development. A person who is not aware of the inauthenticity of his or her condition is likely to feel listless, uncommitted, apathetic, and generally dissatisfied.

In order to be authentic in counseling, advising, and teaching functions, one must be able to understand the six interrelated components of human action within the cultural framework of the person being counseled, advised, or taught. Table One on page 58 gives the values held by a majority of Americans and those held by a contrast-American society. Those groups in the American society that have been most negatively affected by inauthentic institutions, counseling/advising models, and counselors, advisors, and teachers are listed in Table Two, page 60. These groups have been largely neglected because institutional models and approaches have been developed mostly by and for white middle class persons. Cultural influences affecting personality, identity formation, and behavior manifestations are generally not a part of student models. Counseling, advising, and teaching approaches have not always utilized the valuable information derived through examining cultural influences.

In this model, life-span development is comprised of developmental tasks and opportunities from infancy to mature adulthood. Developmental tasks are those things that constitute healthy and satisfactory growth when performed by individuals in society. Opportunities are the moments in which the tasks are optimally achieved (Havighurst, 1967). If a task is not learned at the optimal time, then it may never be learned well. The result may be partial or complete failure in other tasks. Mastery of some tasks results mainly from physical maturation (learning to crawl, walk, etc.). Other tasks are related to social development resulting from cultural expectations and pressure such as social control, personal expression, self-discipline, peer relations, and changes in the personality of the individual as a result of organic and environmental factors.

The developmental tasks from infancy to mature adulthood can be seen in Table III, page 61. Developmental tasks are peculiar to each society and culture. Those presented here are peculiar to the American society. Our focus is on the tasks from adolescence to mature adulthood.

Operation of the Model

Examining the model from one direction reveals that meaning is what prompts human actions. Meaning is the initiator of mission, which directs and focuses action. A sense of mission directs and focuses human energy and power. The use of power moves or modifies personal and social processes and activities. Personal and social power energize and modify social activities. The person acting through the activity structures the action. People behave within the framework of social activities. The personalities and institutional cultures of the people and institutions are resources used to support the individual's lifestyle and social activities. These resources provide the base from which activities occur and are infused. Personalities are the basis of individual human activities; and institutional cultures are the basis of institutional activities.

When examining the model from this perspective, the variables provide direction.

From the other perspective, the variables in the model can be limiting or supporting. For instance, if the sociocultural context, the source from which actions occur, is restricted, then it ultimately will limit human action. A restricted society will limit expansion and development by constraining resources. A restricted personality will cause an individual to experience personal problems and a restricted institutional culture will prevent an institution from performing its functions effectively. When personal and social processes are limiting, they channel power narrowly in limited directions. Through these variables power is enabled.

The exercise of personal power defines goals and purposes, forming a vision of the future, or a mission. Personal power is implemented in the individual's coping strategies and informal activities, and is either expanded or limited by the person's social activities. Socially, if the power is limited, then the accomplishment of goals may be limited. Without a clear sense of direction, a person has a limited reason for being. An unclear mission distorts the meaning system. Similarly, if each variable is supportive, then subsequent variables are enriched, expanded, infused, and energized.

This circular and self-modifying system has feedback loops, which creates the authentic human action system that works for individuals and institutions in any society. The model provides a framework that is comprehensive, as well as diverse in terms of culture and gender. It recognizes the interaction of personal and societal power. It recognizes the flexible and enabling activities for individuals in all cultures and both gender groups. It recognizes the impact of personal and social resources on human actions. It is a valid system that enhances the elements to meet comprehensive human needs; therefore, it is an authentic system. Understanding and knowing the particular elements of culture, class, family background, gender, personal-social attributes, and stage of life-span development, along with expressed and diagnosed problems, enables the system to be descriptive, explanatory, and diagnostic. The mechanism may be used to understand, explain, and prescribe actions to develop and change human functioning over time. Prior to the development of this model, there was no way of looking at, or conceptualizing, authentic multicultural actions in any framework.

Corresponding to this model there are six essential, interrelated questions that need to be examined and answered from both the helper's and the student's perspectives. The answers may vary with individuals and cultures. The questions are:

1. For what reasons do these problematic actions exist?

2. What are the goals and purposes one wishes to achieve?

3. Who is involved (individuals and institutions)? Or what are the energies or driving forces pushing the issues?

4. How are the issues happening? Or how do they operate?

5. What development is needed in personality and what changes are needed in institutional relationships?

6. In what social context does the behavior exist?

After examining the above six questions, the overreaching question, "What interrelationships exist between the issues?" must be answered.

Using these questions as diagnostic mechanisms, and applying the interrelated answers to problems and issues, is the key to preventing problems from emerging, and to resolving unhealthy issues. The teacher must empower the student within the appropriate cultural context. For example, Asian students may view a teacher as an authority and expect directions to be given; therefore, they may not view the relationship as symmetrical and expect any sharing of power. The teacher will have to consider the appropriate intervention for that particular student. The idea is to plan change strategies for each area in the model with the individual in mind. Questions related to implementation of changes are:

1. What changes are necessary in the person's social situation? The smallest unit of analysis is the family, peer group, etc.

2. What changes are necessary in the personality functioning of the individual?

   What changes are necessary in the person's institutional relationships?

   What changes are necessary in the resources with which the person functions?

3. What changes are necessary in the person's personal and social relations and activities?

4. What changes are necessary in the sense and use of power or use of energy?

5. What changes are necessary in the person's directions, goals or purposes?

6. What changes are necessary in the person's meaning systems?

Implications of the Model

No other model of assistance acknowledges the need to work in all six of these dimensions of human action. One implication of this model is that positive roles must be present at every level in developing individuals in the context of any society. The model acknowledges the necessity of various roles for the counselor, advisor, or instructor, in preventing and resolving human problems. The counselor, advisor or instructor's roles are: outreach agent in the community, consultant to the development of a nurturing ecological system, activist and change agent, facilitator of indigenous support systems, advocate, mediator, and professor.

The student also has many roles. Individuals change in the context of many levels of functioning: there are intrapsychic, personality, interpersonal, group, intergroup, social, societal, and cultural changes. Therefore, long-lived change must involve changes along all levels of human functioning. In working toward self-efficacy, individuals need to develop mastery of the continual management of these changes.

A Case Example

CARLOS

Let us suppose that we are dealing with an eighteen-year-old, lower-income, Puerto Rican student from New York City who is a freshman at a large, predominantly white institution in the United States. He is the eldest of three children and the only male from an intact family. His maternal grandmother also lives with the family. He is experiencing problems of adjustment to the college environment; consequently, he has resorted to excessive use of marijuana and alcohol in order to adjust.

Examining the student's problems within the framework of the model, along with an understanding of the student's culture, a counselor may deduce that there are cultural and class conflicts because of the adjustments to the context of the university. Cultural shock may have to be addressed. Within the institutional dimension, Carlos must understand the demands and expectations of the college environment for new behaviors. He is expected to learn a new vocabulary in each subject area and use time differently by being consistently on time for classes, appointments, etc. He is expected to be more assertive in relationships with professors and peers. He is expected to be more independent and self-assured in seeking information and materials to help

himself. The standards of his achievement are different; he needs to know that he is expected to focus on high quality work rather than just work.

Developmental issues may include identity formation, self-concept development, sexual relations, and understanding himself in relation to society -- both predominantly white society and Puerto Rican society. Issues within his family may include a lack of understanding of his experiences in college and appreciation for how he may need to change in order to adjust to the college environment. This lack of understanding by his family members complicates his attempts to maintain relations with them while he adjusts to the university environment. This may create conflicts within himself resulting in alienation from his family and the college environment.

Personality issues to be confronted include those which are due to Carlos' drug and alcohol abuse. He needs to realize the impact of this abuse on his physiological functioning, sensory perceptions and emotions. His feelings about himself, his relationships, and the college environment are likely to have been impacted by his use of alcohol and drugs. He is opting to take drugs and alcohol to feel good rather than taking systematic steps to solve his problems. He has given his personal power over to these forces. He has lost self-discipline and control of the impetus to achieve.

Institutional strategies, community activities, and relationships are part of his problems, thereby related to the solutions to his problems. The student must be assisted in learning the organizational culture: expected relationships, communication patterns and languages, food and eating habits, dress and appearances, values and norms. Carlos must learn how to live in the environment, and master the environment for himself. He must be made to understand the differences between his home environment and the university environment.

Carlos' social interactions, or lack of

interactions, can assist in solving his problems. The press of social power in the community -- power centered in the demands and expectations of Carlos' family, peers, and academic environment -- has acted negatively so far, but there can be a positive side to social power as well. Positive social influence is needed to help Carlos regain self-control and empower him to further change.

In addition, Carlos needs to learn to use the institutional resources available to him: newly-defined support systems of faculty, staff and peers. These can assist him in establishing a new sense of direction, renewing his self-control, and supporting his goals of changing his behavior, feelings and thoughts.

Ultimately, a commitment to a new sense of meaning is necessary. The use and abuse of drugs is indicative of a loss of meaning. Alcoholics Anonymous is successful with many alcoholics because a new creed or philosophy is established. This new belief system creates new meaning.

The particular strategies or interventions must be made peculiar to the problem areas as manifested by Carlos and particular to him. They may involve:

-teaching the required demands and expectations of college;
-advising on alternative courses of actions;
-assisting in securing a health examination;
-reviewing his eating, exercising, and sleeping habits;
-providing support and confirmation regarding the impact of his problems on his self esteem;
-reviewing study habits and attitudes;
-analyzing language skills in Spanish and English;
-exploring family relationships;
-reviewing pleasant sensations, feelings, images, activities, and thoughts in order to focus on successful images, behaviors, and events thus building positive support systems;
-cognitive restructuring in order to change his negative irrational thinking;
-developing new reward systems to support himself; and
-providing bibliotherapy in order to illustrate and to teach the client that he is not the only young Puerto Rican experiencing problems in a predominantly white environment.

He must understand that his predicament is not unique, that it is understandable and changeable. He must feel and experience hope for change in order to deal with continual distress, change his motivations, and help himself learn how to be comfortable in the new social context.

The units of dynamic analysis for any person are the individual interacting in a group (family, peer, etc.) and the influence of the impact of the institutions with which the individual is in contact. It is critically important to look for causes, effects, and interrelationships. Strategies must involve the search for techniques in all dimensions of human action, from the level of the context or existence through resources, to activities, the exercise of power, the pursuit of goals, and the search for meaning.

The above case provides a comprehensive perspective on planned intervention strategies, taking into account the complete human actions of the individual and the anticipated organizational culture of the institution. There are a plurality of problems and issues, therefore meaning intervention strategies must be plural. To be authentic, the questions, intervention strategies, and answers must be personally, socially, and culturally specific. Furthermore, there must be empathy, respect and reciprocal equality in the relationships in the advising/teaching and counseling/therapeutic process whether the relationships are cross-cultural or intracultural (Lazarus, 1979).

The effective counselor, advisor, or instructor maintains this empathy and parity throughout the helping process. The effective person understands the culture, class, gender, and personal issues of the student. An instructor who possesses these skills knows how to give and receive respect, tolerate ambiguity, act non-judgmentally, relate to different persons, and personalize their observations so they're not attributing behavior inaccurately. They must be empathetic, persistent, and reciprocal in relationships and understand various communications styles and languages (Harris and Moran, 1979).

Being effective also requires self-understanding. The instructor needs to know how to effect strategies for the six components relative to himself or herself. He or she needs to expand the response repertoire, and be aware, knowledgeable, and skillful in each area. The response repertoire should cover the full range of human actions to be authentic. One must deal with issues of personal, social, and cultural meanings, missions, power, activities, resources, and the reality of existence in a multicultural or particular cultural context at a particular developmental stage.

Recommendations

The conflict between the student's culture and the culture of the educational institution and the resulting cultural shock must be understood. Understanding the biculturalism that the student must develop to be successful is important.

Faculty need to understand the changes in the curriculum that they must institute so that the students have an environment that is relevant to their needs. They must understand the minority student's general modal personality issues, individual personality, and attempts to adjust in a particular setting. They need to recognize the social processes that are supportive of achievement, and those that are in conflict with individual student's personal goals. Personal/social relationships need to be understood and supported, or helped to change if necessary. Knowing how to assist students to manage their relationships is critically important.

Satisfactory relationships with faculty facilitate the retention of minority students. Faculty are the models, agents of change, mediators, and translators in the college environment. They can help the student establish concrete goals early in their academic career. Even though early goals may be tentative, such as attendance, their establishment is important. They can assist students in understanding the process of the movement toward the achievement of those goals. Students need to know the educational criteria in classes (regarding syllabi, etc.,) and what it takes for movement in the educational process from freshmen to graduate status. Also, students need to be referred to, and faculty need to serve as advocates for, services and resources that help students solve their problems.

Faculty can help students create meaning by helping students develop relationships and commitments to people and ideas within a field of study that leads to the perception that involvement in education is supportive and meaningful. Faculty can create relevant curricula to create the kind of environmental congruence and fit of meaning that students seek.

Faculty must understand authentic behavioral systems as they relate to ethnic minorities in full context, especially noting the specific differences between educational institutions and minority cultural values; the impact of class, ethnicity, and gender on achievement; personal attributes that determine success of minority students; the developmental issues in education; and the organizational culture of the institution. Authenticity resonates with authenticity. Faculty members who are real, concerned, supportive and genuine can make a tremendous difference in the retention of students.

The cultural and gender diversity of faculty and staff needs to be increased. The identification students make with significant others is important in retention. Persons of color need more positive role models who are leaders on campus. The training of more faculty as advisors is important. Persons responsible for the advising structure and process need to ensure that students get to faculty advisors early. Students benefit immensely from the association with faculty in their fields who are competent advisors.

The appropriate classroom conduct, grading practices, and office hours of faculty need to be made clear and should remain consistent. The responsibilities of the professor and students should be made known early in the class. Well stated goals and objectives for each class should be given to students. How the class will be conducted and the method of evaluation (standards, tests, papers, etc.) should be made explicit at the beginning. Also, the faculty needs to know that minority students may not be assertive in coming to their offices. They need to reach out to the students when there is a quizzical look or an apparent lack of attention, when students miss classes for unexplainable reasons, or when students are not participating in their classes.

Mathematics: An Example

A concrete illustration of these principles for faculty involvement can be given in the area of mathematics. Many students do not perform well in mathematics. Success in mathematics is essential for minority student retention in the sciences.

A suggested class structure in the difficult area of math is the following:

1. Specify the course outline and objectives for the mathematical operations to be learned.

2. Have the students verbalize the operational processes associated with solving each problem.

3. Work in groups to solve problems; ensure that each student can work all the problems while in the group and when he or she is alone.

4. Develop a communications network among and between students (distribute a list of telephone numbers and encourage their use).

5. Use a cognitive process through which the students learn from the professor and from each other. Use an interactive learning model.

6. Have the students raise these questions and answers in solving problems:

   -What does it mean or for what reasons?
   -For what purposes?
   -What is the idea or driving force behind these mathematical operations?
   -What are the processes to be used?
   -What is needed?
   -In what context or situation does this exist or should this be used?
   -Computational skills must serve a purpose to be able to be understood. It is important to understand and to choose the correct processes that serve a particular situation.

7. Give frequent assessments and positive, corrective, specific feedback on skills, processes, and answers.

8. Create active involvement in classroom and laboratory sessions. Classes should be problem-solving sessions including both the students and the professors.

9. Use the history of math as a motivator and developer of confidence.

10. Do not limit expectations! Heighten expectations! At least 60% of the class should get A's with this new methodology! Tell them you expect A's and believe it!

11. Serve as a translator, mediator, and model in the classroom.

12. Listen to students' use of language to recognize learning styles, and facilitate language that correctly states problems, processes, etc.; and

note language that mitigates against learning.
Language differences often interfere with
learning because of misunderstanding. There is
interference (conflict) and dominance (one
language use over another).

Faculty members taking an active role of leadership and working on the resolution of students'
problems, while recognizing activities in all six
dimensions of human activities, can make significant differences in the retention and development of
minority students. Presently, America is moving
backward -- not forward -- in its efforts to achieve
full participation of minority citizens in the life
and prosperity of higher education (ACE, 1989).
Faculty members at institutions of higher education can make a difference in reversing this trend.

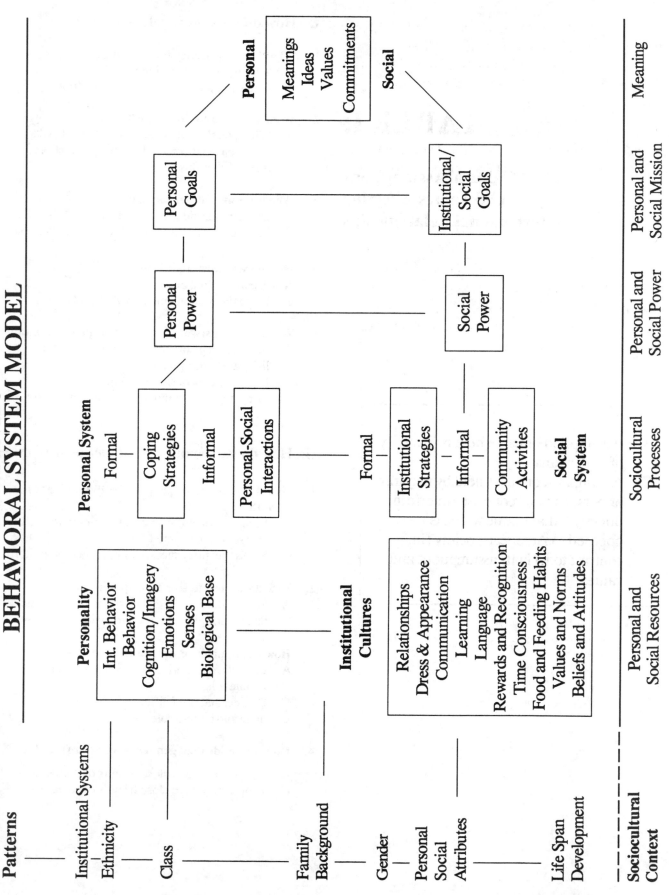

AUTHENTIC BEHAVIORAL SYSTEM MODEL

TABLE I:

Cultural Assumptions and Values Affecting Interpersonal Relationships

```
A = Assumption or value held by majority
    of Americans
C = Assumption or value held by majority
    of persons of a "contrast-American
    Society"; that is, one which is
    opposed to American society (in
    contrast to it) in its assumptions and
    values.
```

I. How do we see ourselves?

1. **What is our primary identification?**
    A Within ourselves as individuals
    C As part of a family, clan, caste, or tribe

2. **What do we value in people?**
    A What people can achieve with special skills
    C A person's background, family connections, tribal affiliations

3. **Whom do we rely on for help?**
    A Ourselves as independent and resourceful
    C Friends, family and others owing us obligations

4. **How do we learn about life?**
    A From personal experience
    C From the wisdom and knowledge of others

5. **What is the basis of social control in a community?**
    A From feelings of guilt because we are not living up to our personal standard
    C From feelings of shame because we are not living up to the standards of our community

II. How do we see our relationships with others?

1. **How do we relate to people of different status or authority?**
    A Minimize the difference; take for granted everyone's the same
    C Stress the differences; show respect for authority

2. **How do we relate to new acquaintances?**
    A Stress informality; make people feel at home
    C Stress formality; act properly with strangers

3. **How do we idealize work and sex roles?**
    A Little differentiation between male and female roles
    C Distinct and rigid differentiation between male and female roles

4. **How do we idealize gender in relationships?**
    A People may have close friends of both sexes
    C People may have close friends of same sex

5. **How do we idealize sex roles in relationships?**
   A   Sex equality for males and females
   C   Male superiority

6. **What are our loyalties to organizational life?**
   A   Move easily from one organization to another when our personal goals are not fulfilled
   C   Remain with our organization from sense of loyalty even when goals are not fulfilled

7. **What are the characteristics of friendship?**
   A   A loose concept applied to many people and based on overlapping special interests; limited obligations to one another
   C   A specific concept applied to a few people; total involvement based upon mutual love and respect; unlimited obligations to one another.

8. **How do we deal with conflict?**
   A   Favor eye-to-eye confrontation
   C   Find it unacceptable and embarrassing

9. **How do we regard kidding or joking at the expense of others?**
   A   As acceptable, interesting and fun
   C   As unacceptable and embarrassing

10. **How do we interact socially?**
    A   Do things together
    C   Be together

11. **What is the preferred pace of life?**
    A   Fast, busy, conducive to getting things done
    C   Slow, steady, getting the most from life

III. How do we see the world?

1. **What is nature like?**
   A   Physical; knowable by scientific investigation
   C   Spiritual and mystical

2. **How do natural forces in the world operate?**
   A   In a rational, controllable manner
   C   In a predetermined, spiritually controlled manner

3. **What is the role of fate in life?**
   A   Little influence; we are masters of our destiny
   C   Great influence; no power to alter it

4. **What is our relationship with nature?**
   A   Modify nature for our needs
   C   Integrate with the natural forces around us

5. **What is our attitude toward what we desire in life?**
   A   What is good or desired is unlimited if we work hard
   C   What is good or desired is limited and must be shared with others

6. **How do we look at time?**
   A   In precise minutes and hours by which we organize our days
   C   In diffuse days, weeks or months by which we organize our years

7. **How do we value time?**
   A   As a limited resource not to be wasted
   C   As an unlimited resource to be used

8. **How does life unfold?**
   A   In a lineal fashion through history
   C   In a cyclical fashion through recurring seasonal patterns

9. **How do we measure progress?**
   A   In concrete, quantifiable units which indicate amount, size, percent, and the like
   C   Against abstract social and moral principles or our society

10. **On what basis do we make decisions?**
    A   Will it work?
    C   Is it right?

-- Rhinesmith, 1975

TABLE II:

Cultural Groups and Relevant Cultural Varibles Related to the Unfulfilled Promise of Life in America

Cultural Groups in USA

African-Americans	Jamaicans
Haitians	Puerto Ricans
Cubans	Dominicans
Mexican-Americans	South American Immigrants
Chinese-Americans	Japanese-Americans
Vietnamese	Hmong
Cambodians	Filipinos
American Indians (numerous nations and tribes)	

Cultural Variables

Character and Personality
Communication and Language
Dress and Appearance
Food and Feedhabits
Time and Time Consciousness
Rewards and Recognitions
Relationships
Values and Norms
Sense of Self and Space
Mental Processes and Learning
Beliefs and Attitudes
Family Organization (roles of the family and its
    individual members)
Activity Orientation (being and doing)
Perception of Society
Interpersonal Orientation: (listening, body-orientation,
    spatial relations, touching orientation, eye behavior)
Nature of Self-disclosure
Nature of Humankind to Nature
Perceptions of Health and Unhealthiness
How Stress is Experienced and Manifested
Social Behavior (formality or informality)
Perceptions of Age and Aging
Developmental Stages in Society
How Social Control is Exerted
Socialization Processes
Concepts of Work

TABLE III:

Developmental Tasks

Developmental Tasks of Infancy and Early Childhood

1. Learning to walk
2. Learning to take solid foods
3. Learning to talk
4. Learning to control the elimination of body wastes
5. Learning sex differences and sexual modesty
6. Achieving physiological stability
7. Performing simple concepts of social and physical reality
8. Learning to relate oneself emotionally to parents, siblings, and other people
9. Learning to distinguish right and wrong and developing a conscience

Developmental Tasks of Middle Childhood

1. Learning physical skills necessary for ordinary games
2. Building wholesome attitudes toward oneself as a growing organism
3. Learning to get along with age-mates
4. Learning an appropriate masculine or feminine social role
5. Developing fundamental skills in reading, writing, and calculating
6. Developing concepts necessary for everyday living
7. Developing conscience, morality, and a scale of values
8. Achieving personal independence
9. Developing attitudes toward social groups and institutions

Development Tasks of Adolescence

1. Achieving new and more relations with age-mates of both sexes
2. Achieving a masculine or feminine social role
3. Accepting one's physique and using the body effectively
4. Achieving emotional independence of parents and other adults
5. Achieving assurance of economic independence
6. Selecting and preparing for an occupation
7. Preparing for marriage and family life
8. Developing intellectual skills and concepts necessary for civic competence
9. Desiring and achieving socially responsible behavior
10. Acquiring a set of values and an ethical system as guide to behavior

Developmental Tasks of Early Adulthood

1. Selecting a mate
2. Learning to live with a marriage partner
3. Starting a family
4. Rearing children
5. Managing a home
6. Getting started in an occupation
7. Taking on civic responsibility
8. Finding a congenial social group

Developmental Tasks of Middle Age

1. Achieving adult civic and social responsibility
2. Establishing and maintaining an economic standard of living
3. Assisting teenage children to be more responsible and happy adults
4. Developing adult leisure-time activities
5. Relating oneself to one's spouse as a person
6. Accepting and adjusting to the physiological changes of middle age
7. Adjusting to aging parents

Developmental Tasks of Late Maturity

1. Adjusting to decreasing physical strength and health
2. Adjustment to retirement and reduced income
3. Adjusting to death of spouse
4. Establishing an explicit affiliation with one's age group
5. Meeting social and civic obligations
6. Establishing satisfactory physical living arrangements

(Havinghurst, 1967)

References

American College Testing. (1979). *Why Students Stay, Why They Leave, What Makes the Difference.*

American Council on Education. (1988). *One Third of a Nation.*

Astin, Alexander W. (1982). *Four Critical Years.* San Francisco: Jossey-Bass.

Astin, Alexander W. (1985). *Achieving Educational Excellence.* San Francisco: Jossey-Bass.

Avakian, N.A., MacKinney, A.C., and Allen, Glenn R. (1982). "Race and Sex Differences in Student Retention at an Urban University College and University." Winter, 160-165.

Etzioni, Amitai. (1968). *The Active Society.* New York: The MacMillan Company.

Havighurst, Robert J. (1967). *Developmental Tasks in Education.* New York: David McKay.

Harris, Philip R. & Moran, Robert T. (1979). *Managing Cultural Differences.* Houston: Gulf.

Lazurus, Arnold. (1979). *Multimodal Therapy.* Kingston, New Jersey: Multimodal Therapy Institute, May 11-13.

Sedlacek, W.E. and Brooks, G.C. (1982). *The Use of Nontraditional Predictors for Admissions to the University of Maryland.* College Park Press.

Rhinesmith, Stephen H. (1975). *Bring Home the World.* AMACOM.

Stikes, C.S. (1984). *Black Students in Higher Education.* Carbondale: Southern IL Univ. Press.

Stikes, C.S. (1989). *A Model for an Authentic Human Action System: Implications for Counseling and Therapy.* Paper presented at the Annual Meeting of the American Association for Counseling and Development, Boston, MA.

Tinto, V. (1987). *Leaving College.* Chicago: The University of Chicago Press.

TWO PROGRAMS TO INVOLVE FACULTY

In Retention
Initiatives

by
Dr. Charles
Taylor

Faculty have more power to improve minority student retention than any other group on campus. The key is to convince faculty to become involved in retention activities. Two programs that have met with success in increasing faculty minority student interaction are faculty-student mentor programs and faculty early warning programs. Both are described in detail in the pages that follow. Use them as a guide to establish your own.

FACULTY-STUDENT MENTOR PROGRAM

The goal of the mentor program is to enable students to relate with a professional person on campus under informal and non-threatening circumstances. Ideally, friendships will develop in such a way that students feel comfortable in approaching their mentors for help with academic, social, and personal concerns.

Objectives

1. To foster a relationship in which the student feels that there is someone on the faculty who cares about his or her academic success, and to whom he or she can turn when the need arises.

2. To sensitize more faculty, staff, and administrators to important issues that face minority students on the campus.

3. To assist students in adjusting to campus life.

4. To foster minority student retention by creating an atmosphere where students and teachers reclaim their supportive roles.

5. To assist students in finding both on- and off-campus services, as appropriate.

Program Structure

It is recommended that a mentor program coordinator be selected to administer the program. This person should be responsible for all parts of the program. This person will be responsible for adhering to the following structure:

A. He or she should attempt to match faculty, staff, and administrators whose academic specialty or interest is similar to their assigned student's major.

B. When a prospective mentor specifies the gender of student he or she would prefer to work with, the program shall make every effort to accommodate the request.

C. Students accepted into the program should be either first-semester freshmen or new transfer students. Other students who may request a mentor can be included only if there are adequate resources and their participation does not jeopardize new freshmen participation. In every instance, participation should be voluntary.

D. At the beginning of each semester, the mentor program coordinator should hold an orientation meeting for new students and their mentors. Afterwards, mentors and students are expected to meet at least monthly during the school year.

E. The mentor program coordinator is expected to stay in regular contact with mentors and students. Any formal written correspondence between the mentor and coordinator should be carried out in a professional manner. All questions and complaints are to be addressed as they arise.

F. If appointments cannot be kept, the person experiencing a conflict is expected to notify the other in advance of the arranged date. Students who consistently fail to meet with their mentors should be dropped from the program. In those instances where the match-up between mentor and student does not appear to be working, the coordinator will be responsible for ending the relationship and making new assignments where possible.

The mentor program can improve its credibility and faculty acceptance a great deal by having the coordinator attend faculty departmental meetings to explain the program first-hand. The coordinator should also get on the Dean's Council agenda to solicit their endorsement of the program. Similarly, the coordinator should meet with new minority student freshmen and transfer students to explain the program to them as well. By meeting with both mentors and students beforehand, the chances of program success are enhanced.

During the meeting with potential mentors, the program coordinator should pass out information sheets and application forms. Faculty will probably raise a number of questions and the information sheet will answer the vast majority of them. Typically, questions center around how students are selected and what is expected of the mentor. It is recommended that the program maintain a high level of informality. The fastest way to kill faculty enthusiasm is to add another level of bureaucracy. If possible, require no paperwork and no reporting, and strive to make the program as hassle-free as possible.

After faculty have returned their application forms, the coordinator should follow up with phone calls to obtain additional information about the mentors that will help him or her make an appropriate match, as well as share information about the mentor with students. The coordinator should obtain information about the mentor's preference for movies and social activities, academic interests, gender of student preferred, etc.

Mentors should be informed that while they are able to discriminate by sex, they cannot do so by race. While it's acceptable for a female mentor to want to interact with a female student, the race of the student cannot be decided by the mentor.

When there is considerable faculty support, the coordinator may find him or herself in the enviable position of having more mentors than students requesting mentors. When this situation occurs, some type of screening process may have to be implemented. However, it may be wise to permit mentor teams (two faculty members) or assign mentors for one semester only, or establish a waiting list. Ironically, a waiting list in this program adds to its prestige. It implies strong support for the program and sends a positive signal to minority students. When screening of mentors cannot be avoided, make sure it is done in a sensitive fashion. Unfortunately, there is no agreed-upon scientific method that shows beforehand who will make a good mentor. Often the people we prejudge as less than ideal candidates for mentorship surprise us and end up receiving the highest praise from students. Your pre-screen questions may help flag potential problems, but keep in mind these "matches" are not made in heaven. The decision to exclude someone should be based primarily on whether he or she will meet the objectives of the program. The mentor's reasons for wanting to be a mentor may also be helpful in the screening process.

After the screening is completed and the roster of mentors is filled in, the coordinator will need to begin the process of matching mentors and students. Before the matching is done, it is assumed that the coordinator has already met with both groups. It is also assumed that the coordinator has obtained enough information to help both the mentor and student break the ice. While information about the mentors will come from the application forms and follow-up phone calls, it is recommended that information about the students come from the student survey (see page 39). This survey can be very useful in providing an academic and social "profile" of students. Mentors will know immediately what movies, music, and speakers students prefer. It will also be evident in which academic areas students will need assistance.

When the mentor-student match is made on paper, the coordinator is ready to inform both parties and call a general orientation meeting. The orientation meeting should be held off-campus if possible. If that cannot be arranged, hold the meeting in the student union or some other informal setting. The coordinator should impress upon everyone that this is an informal program that stresses personal interaction. The coordinator should mention the importance of keeping dates and showing up on time. She or he should discuss the type of activities students are interested in generally. It should be mentioned that, at a minimum, monthly meetings are required, but that weekly or biweekly meetings are preferred. After a question-and-answer period, there should be ample time left for mentors and students to interact. Human-relation activities can be used during orientation to help mentors and students become comfortable with one another. When the meeting is over, every mentor and student should have set a date for their next meeting.

Monitoring

The coordinator's role now shifts to monitoring the program. While the mentors or students are not required to complete any paperwork, it is important for the coordinator to keep good records. The coordinator should have a master sheet that includes mentor and student addresses and telephone numbers. Records should be kept of any contact with mentors and students, and of the types of activities in which the mentors and students have engaged. Records should be kept on whether activities reported are of an academic or social nature. Through appropriate monitoring, the coordinator can nip potential troublespots in the bud. He or she can contact mentors or students who repeatedly miss appointments, and serve as a mediator when appropriate.

Conflict

Occasionally, a situation arises in which the mentor and student turn out to be incompatible. The coordinator should talk to each party separately to find out what caused the incompatibility. If the situation cannot be reconciled, an attempt should be made to find other matches.

Year-End Activity

Prior to the semester's end, the coordinator should put together an ad-hoc committee comprised of mentors and students to plan a year-end activity. This could be a picnic, a weekend retreat, or similar social gathering. There should be time allotted for mentors and students to tell what the program has meant to them. The year-end activity should culminate the program for that semester.

Funding

It is not necessary to create a full-time coordinator position to administer this program. It can be run out of your existing Minority Affairs Office, depending of course on the size of the office. A graduate student or senior workstudy student can be assigned to the program. Duties can be assigned to existing staff as well. Essentially, a substantial amount of time is needed to set up the program and get it off the ground. Once it is running, less time is required for monitoring. Additional funding should be allocated for supplies, phone calls, and refreshments for the orientation and year-end activity. Overall, the mentor program represents an inexpensive method for impacting minority student retention in a positive manner. Faculty are involved directly in retention initiatives in a personal way.

Evaluation

Evaluation of the program can occur at the year-end activity, depending on the type of evaluation your program selects. The coordinator can develop a traditional evaluation form based on the program's objectives, and have participants complete it. By analyzing the results, he or she will have a better picture of how the program was perceived and know what its strengths and weaknesses were. The coordinator should perform a self-evaluation as well, noting aspects of the program that worked well along with those aspects which need improvement. She or he should determine how many mentors and students continued their relationship beyond the academic year. If your program has adequate resources, consider performing a study to test your hypothesis that the mentor program contributes to new minority student retention. The

point in all of this is to stress the need for an annual evaluation. By doing so, the program stands a greater chance of being around on your campus for many years.

Sample of letter to solicit Faculty support

Memorandum

To: Deans and Department Heads
From: Mentor Program Coordinator
Date:
Re: Faculty-Student Mentor Program

The purpose of this memo is to share information and to seek your support for a new Faculty-Student Mentor program our office hopes to implement during the 1990-91 academic year.

The Mentor program matches faculty and staff with new Minority freshmen and transfer students. The program is completely voluntary and is intended to directly involve faculty and staff in helping Minority students adjust to campus and to the surrounding community.

The enclosed information sheet explains the program in greater detail. As you will see there is as little red tape as possible. To get involved all one needs to do is fill out an application form. It has been my experience that many faculty want to assist in making the environment more hospitable for Minority students. The Mentor program may be an ideal way for them to do so.

Similar programs on other campuses have found mentors and students participating in outings, home visits and a host of community activities. However, what may be equally important is that the Mentor program has proven quite successful in helping retain Minority students.

Please circulate the enclosed flyers and encourage faculty and staff to get involved. I look forward to being placed on your next staff meeting agenda to answer questions about the program in greater detail. In the interim, please refer all questions about the program to me. Thank you.

Cover letter for Mentor Program

Dear _____
　　　　　name of Mentor

Thank your for your interest in becoming a Mentor. Attached is an information sheet explaining the program. We welcome your involvement and support with this new initiative.

With your participation we believe minority student freshmen stand a good chance of succeeding both socially and academically this year. We're excited about the Mentor Program and we hope you will be, too.

I will contact you shortly to explain the program in greater detail and assign you a student, and then have you take it from there.

I would also like to call you occasionally to see how things are going and to inform you about semester activities for Mentors and Students. If you have questions now or in the future, don't hesitate to call.

With best regards,

Mentor Program Coordinator

P.S. There will be an orientation meeting for students and mentors at:

_____

(time, date, place)

Please plan to attend.

Faculty/Student Mentor Program Information Sheet

What it is

The Mentor program is a new initiative that matches Mentors (faculty or staff members) with Minority students. Mentors contact the students when they arrive on campus, welcome them to the community, and serve as their mentor during their first year on campus. The initial program will concentrate on new freshmen only. When the program is evaluated in the summer, a decision will be made whether to expand it to other students or not.

Who can participate?

Mentors volunteer by contacting the Mentor Program Coordinator. They can be faculty, staff, or community adults who are committed to cultural pluralism and helping students adjust to a predominantly white campus. An information sheet is sent to interested individuals and an application form is included. Potential mentors are asked to return the application, and staff will contact them shortly thereafter.

How are the Mentors and Students matched?

The office maintains a list of new minority freshmen as well as a list of Mentors. Staff match the lists according to interest, majors, and or requests. The Mentor Program Coordinator interviews Mentors about student preference. While Mentors cannot select the race of the student they will be involved with, they can select the gender.

What if the match doesn't work?

Let's face it. Not all relationships are compatible no matter how well the intentions. In those rare cases, staff will discuss the situation with both parties individually, and if the differences can't be resolved, simply end the relationship.

Mentors can be assigned another student, and vice-versa, if available.

Is any reporting or monitoring required?

The program is not intended to create another layer of bureaucracy, so no formal reports are required. However, we would like to be kept informed of activities you engage the student in so those ideas can be shared with other Mentors. During the first year, we would also like to know about how many times you contacted the student. Finally, we would like to select a mentor from time to time to feature in our monthly newsletter or campus newspaper, so we may periodically contact you.

Will Mentors get a chance to interact with other Mentors and Students?

An end-of-the-year activity will be planned for all Mentors and students. Mentors are also free to plan such activities, and the Mentor Coordinator will help plan group activities.

How long am I expected to be a Mentor?

We ask that you serve as a Mentor for one academic year (September-May). You can participate in subsequent years if you're still interested.

What's expected of Mentors?

Mentors are expected to meet with the student initially and to contact the student on a regular basis throughout the semester. Activities, outings, etc., are at the discretion of the mentor and student. At least once during the semester, it's recommended that you invite the student on some type of outing.

What's expected of students?

Students are expected to meet with the mentor and to initiate some of the contact as well.

What type of orientation do Mentors and Students receive?

The mentor coordinator will interview each Mentor and student and inform them of the program's expectations. Following the interview, there will be a general orientation where the goals and expectations are discussed in greater detail. The Mentor Program Coordinator will provide assistance as needed throughout the year.

Annual Evaluation

We'll ask students and Mentors to fill out an evaluation at the end of the academic year to access the program and make recommendations on how it can be improved.

Do I need any special training?

No, all you need is the desire to help students adjust to the collegiate community.

Who will be my contact person throughout the year?

The Mentor Program Coordinator, who can be reached at (include home and campus phone and addresses).

How do I sign up?

Complete the attached application form and send it to the Mentor Program Coordinator at

_____
(address)
or call _____
(phone #)
if you have questions or need additional information.

Faculty-Student Mentor Application Form

__ Yes, I am interested in becoming a Mentor. I am able to serve for one academic year. I have read the information sheet and agree to its conditions. I understand the Mentor Program Coordinator will contact me.

_____
Name

_____
Campus Department/Office

_____
Campus Phone #

_____
Home Address

Briefly explain below why you are interested in the Mentor program, what you hope to get out of the program, and what you hope to contribute.

Return this application to:

(address of appropriate office here)

FACULTY EARLY WARNING SYSTEM

While the mentor program's emphasis is on the social well-being of the student, the Faculty Early Warning System concentrates on the student's academic well-being. This program has great potential when administered appropriately. It attempts to build an academic partnership between faculty, minority students, and Minority Affairs staff.

The program is normally administered through the Minority Affairs office or Academic Advisor's office. It has experienced its greatest success at smaller institutions, but many larger universities have experienced success with it as well. You can concentrate on the freshmen class or the entire minority student body, depending on its size. The program is excellent for special services programs. Since many of the record-keeping functions are computerized, the class size is less important.

After you determine your roster of students who will be included in the program, it is recommended that a meeting be held with the registrar's office. The registrar can advise you on the best way to access student records and class schedules. He or she can also advise on a simple computer program to match the names from your roster with their professors. You will need the names of your roster's professors to launch your program. You will need to access the program the registrar sets up for you five to six weeks after classes start, midterm, and at the end of the semester. This will allow you to monitor student grades and make contact with professors as needed.

You will have to sell this program to the faculty as well. Keep in mind that faculty traditionally resist any program that requires a lot of time or is perceived as being bureaucratic. Keep your program simple and demonstrate to faculty how the program will assist them, and you stand a better chance of gaining their support. In order to cultivate faculty support, it is recommended that you get placed on the Deans and Department heads agendas. This will give you a chance to introduce yourself and your program directly. You will be able to answer questions and test how receptive faculty are to the programs. At these meetings, you should be able to find out how soon in the semester faculty test students and how often they give out assignments. This information will help you determine how often you will need to receive the faculty early warning student monitoring form. Ideally, you would receive feedback from faculty at least thrice during the semester: After the fifth or sixth week of class; after mid-term; and after the semester is over. Some faculty won't test until mid-term, so it is important to talk with students about keeping up with class assignments in that situation.

After you've identified your roster and set up meetings to explain your program to the faculty, send them information about the program. Information should cover the purpose of the program, a copy of forms faculty will need to complete, and information on how the program will be monitored. Be sure to send students listed on your roster information as well. It is highly recommended that you hold a meeting for students to explain the program and answer questions they may have.

How the Program Works

Obtain a list of the professors of students enrolled in the program from the registrar's office. By the fifth week after classes start, send faculty a copy of the Faculty Early Warning System Student Monitoring Form. Have faculty return this form directly to you. Encourage faculty to complete the entire form even if they are unable to answer some of the questions. Pay special attention to the comments faculty write. They can be very instructive when advising students.

When you have received the forms from faculty you and your staff will need to set up meetings with students to review the reports. We've found that students respond positively to being able to review their progress early in the semester. Below is a sample memo that you can send to students to discuss the reports.

To: All Students enrolled in
            Faculty Early Warning Program
From:
Date:
Re: Faculty Early Warning Reports

As you know, we are working with your teachers to monitor your academic progress. Early in the semester we sent out Faculty Early Warning reports to all of your teachers. Their reports can help give you and us a better idea of how well you are doing in your classes, or warn us that you may need to find ways to improve your grades. The responses have been pouring in from your teachers and should prove to be quite helpful. In order for these reports to be useful to you, please make an appointment to see me and discuss your reports. Thank you.

During the counselor-student meeting, the counselor or advisor should carefully review the student's progress in the class. When the student is doing well, that should be acknowledged. When the student is having difficulty, remedies should be explored. These remedies should be agreed upon in writing by the student, counselor, and teacher. After the counselor has met with the student, the student should then set up a meeting with his or her teacher to discuss the remedies suggested. The teacher may add remedies. He or she should then sign the *Remedies Form*. A copy of this form should go to the teacher, student, and counselor.

An example of a Remedies Form

Name of Student _____

ID Number _____

Course _____

Time/Day_____

Instructor_____

After meeting with the student the following suggestions were agreed upon to help improve the student's classroom performance

_____ Attending classes

_____ Taking notes

_____ Study skills sessions

_____ Tutoring

_____ Regular counseling

_____ Other _____

_____

_____

The student has agreed to take the following steps to address the items checked above: _____

_____

_____

Student signature _____

Counselor/advisor signature _____

Instructor_____

Other comments:

_____ Student has dropped the course.

_____ Student plans to drop the course.

_____ Other _____

_____

_____

As another check and to encourage students to meet with their teachers, it is advisable to send a follow-up letter to teachers similar to the following.

MEMO

To: (name of instructor)
From:
Re: Faculty Early Warning Report
Date:

We would like to express our appreciation to you for completing the Faculty Early Warning Report forms. Your efforts have helped us identify some academic problems early enough to allow us to address them. (Name of student) has come in to discuss your feedback on his (or her) progress. We have encouraged him (or her) to set up an appointment with you, whether or not there is a problem, but especially if there is a problem. In addition, we have suggested the remedies on the enclosed form as a way of helping the student improve his (or her) academic standing in your class. Please discuss this (or other) remedy(ies) as you see fit. Then please sign the form and return a copy to my office.

We will be closely monitoring the student's progress for the remainder of the semester. We have made it clear to the student that the ultimate responsibility for succeeding academically in your class is up to him (or her). Again, thank you for your assistance. Feel free to contact me to discuss this further.

cc: Student File

The above scenario should be repeated after mid-term and at the end of the semester. An important caveat to keep in mind is that when advising students, counselors should attempt to have the following information available:

1) Student transcripts
2) Test scores
3) Faculty Early Warning Report
4) Course syllabi
5) Course descriptions and reading lists
6) Tutorial information

At the end of the semester, it's important to get faculty feedback on how the Early Warning System worked out and how it can be improved upon. After the first time around, faculty are usually more receptive. It doesn't hurt to send a final thank you letter at the end of the semester to faculty, department chairs, and college deans.

Involve Parents

Many institutions are finding if they involve parents, the Faculty Early Warning System is strengthened further. Students should be given the option of involving their parents, however it's been our experience that parental involvement works well with freshmen students, but upperclass students tend to reject it.

Example of an
Faculty Early Warning System
Student Monitoring Form

Student Name _____

ID # _____

Course/Section _____

Instructor _____

Date Sent _____

Please rate this student by using the following scale:

Excellent	Good	Fair	Poor	Very Poor	Unable to Answer
1	2	3	4	5	6

_____ Participates in class discussions

_____ Attendance

_____ Submits assignments on time

_____ Quality of homework assignments submitted

_____ Quiz results

_____ Test results

_____ Asks for assistance if having difficulty

_____ Explanation of items checked _____

_____

_____

What grade would you assign this student at this time?
(circle one) A A/B B B/C C D F Other ____

Comments:

Please return this form to:

   (Address)

Call _____ if you have questions or need additional information.

Improving Academic Skills:
The Grambling Developmental Education Model

ABOUT THE AUTHOR:

Dr. Lamore J. Carter

Dr. Carter is Vice President for Academic Affairs and Research, Coordinator of Consent Decree Compliance, and Professor of Psychology and Education at Grambling State University. Carter earned his B.A. Degree in Zoology from Fisk University in Nashville, Tennessee; received his M.S. Degree in Educational Psychology and Science Methods from the University of Wisconsin at Madison, Wisconsin; the Ph.D. Degree in Psychology (Educational/Experimental) from the State University of Iowa, Iowa City; and did post-doctoral work at Harvard University. He has also served as Distinguished Visiting Professor at Morehouse College; earned a post-doctoral fellowship in Education Research with the Commission on Colleges, Southern Association of Colleges and Schools(SACS), Atlanta, Georgia;

served as Dean of Faculty at Texas Southern University; and was an American Council of Education Fellow in Academic Administration at Louisiana State University.

Dr. Carter's consultative work has emphasized psychology as applied to learning and behavior of children, youth, and adults; and evaluation and accreditation in higher education. He has served for twenty-five years as a Vocational Expert and Consulting Psychologist for the Bureau of Hearings and Appeals of the Social Security Administration, and for twenty years as a regular consultant for the Commission on Colleges-SACS. He has travelled extensively across the United States, Canada, Europe, Mexico, Africa, South America and the Far East doing consultative and business work .

INTRODUCTION

Grambling State University's Developmental Education Program (DEP) targets students who have received low ACT scores and enrolls them in remedial coursework, which must be completed before the major field of study may be entered. The program is comprehensive, comprised of courses in English, Mathematics, and Reading, and includes counseling and tutoring. The program is highly structured.

This paper describes the goals and administration of Grambling's DEP, details how students are identified and served, and lists the requisites for entering and exiting the DEP. The program emphasis is on progression; students are not labeled as disadvantaged, but as developmental. The students receive a periodic evaluation while enrolled in the program, and data is kept on the progress of individual students as well as on the overall efficacy of the program in promoting successful student retention.

IMPROVING ACADEMIC SKILLS:

The Grambling Developmental Education Model

by
Lamore J.
Carter, Ph.D.

Studies have indicated that developmental education programs are effective for students with ACT composite scores of less than 16. There are now pilot or long-standing programs at most of the thirty-five traditionally Black public colleges and Black private schools which have had Title III-- Developing Institutions Grants.

In Grambling State University's Comprehensive Developmental Education Program (DEP), all students with composite ACT scores of 15 or less are designated as developmental students and are required to enter and exit the program in order to enter a major field of study.

Developmental Education Student is a label we use to identify students who have entrance test scores in communicative and/or computational skills which are at a level we judge to be too low for the student to negotiate the regular curriculum unless special instructional and counseling assistance is provided.

Developmental Education Program is a term we use to designate the special instructional and counseling services provided for developmental education students and the training enhancement of the faculty who teach and counsel developmental education students.

The American College Testing (ACT) Program scores are used initially for placement of students. To further establish the validity of intended placement, the University administers diagnostic tests in basic skills areas. Scores from these tests are correlated with ACT scores to determine if there are significant differences. When significant differences occur, students are counseled on an individual basis to determine actual placement.

The program is comprehensive, comprised of remedial courses in English, mathematics, and reading; and of instructional support systems, academic skills courses, counseling and tutoring. It is highly structured with some flexibility in meeting the needs of students. Experimental studies have indicated that highly structured development programs offer the greatest chances for success. Our program conforms with suggestions and specifications adopted by the Developmental Education Task Force of the Louisiana Board of Regents and with specifications of such programs adopted by the Board of Regents.

I. Objectives of the Program

A. To provide a comprehensive, highly structured program to build the basic skills essential to success in college.

B. To allow a period of one semester or more for underprepared students (those with low ACT scores) to become acclimated to college standards before enrolling in the basic core courses.

C. To provide special supportive services for underprepared students through special academic support systems, counseling and tutoring on a needs basis.

D. To provide basic skills courses with an environment conducive to learning through small classes, media support systems and individualized assistance.

E. To maximize the students' chances for success at Grambling State University.

II. Program Administration

The entire developmental program at the University level is under the direction of a director who manages, supervises, and coordinates the various components of the program and facilitates coordination among personnel. Each component has a coordinator, who is responsible to an academic department head and the program director, and also responsible for frequent communication with departmental faculties, especially English and mathematics. This facilitates maximum departmental involvement and complete integration of the program and its faculty/staff into the University system. The faculty, counselors, coordinators, and director are required to meet on a regularly scheduled basis for program coordination and discussion of program progress as well as for program planning.

III. Identification of Students

All students with ACT individual mathematics and English scores of less than 16 are involved in this program. Students who fail to score at the 11th grade proficiency level on the Nelson-Denny Reading test are required to become involved in this program. Students with higher ACT scores (16-19) will also be involved if need is evident. Students with ACT composite scores of less than 16 are further tested in English and mathematics to assure accuracy in testing and placement of students in the Developmental Education Program. Each student is counseled as to the intent and objectives of this program as well as the need for his or her participation.

Academic Load for DEP Students

A student placed in two or more DEP courses is limited to a maximum course load of thirteen (13) credit hours during a regular semester and seven credit hours during a 9-week summer session.

A student placed in only one DEP course is permitted to carry a maximum load of fifteen (15) hours during a regular semester and nine credit hours during a 9-week summer session.

A student placed in a DEP course is permitted to begin enrolling in courses for a major which accepts freshman enrollment, but the student must complete all DEP courses before being permitted to take a full load of college credit bearing courses.

Credit

The Developmental Education courses at Grambling State University are designed for credit and the traditional grading system, with the additional grade of NC (No Credit), is used.

However, credit for developmental education courses are used to fulfill graduation requirements.

IV. Academic Components of the Program

A. English Instruction

Developmental English is required for students who score less than 16 on the ACT English Section and students who fail to demonstrate adequate writing skills. Each student is given an opportunity to test out of Developmental English. A grade of "C" or better is required for enrollment in the regular English course.

B. Mathematics Instruction

Developmental Math is required for students who score less than 16 on the ACT Math Section. Each student is given an opportunity to test out of Developmental Math in the first class section. Students are required to pass a departmental test to proceed to the regular Math course.

C. Reading Instruction

Developmental Reading is required for all students who failed to achieve a 12th grade level reading proficiency (total score) on the Nelson-Denny tests. Students achieving a grade level above 12 are allowed to test out of Developmental Reading. Students are required to demonstrate adequate reading proficiency before they are allowed to exit Developmental Reading.

D. Academic Skills Instruction

A course designed to provide students with basic college orientation, personal adjustments, study techniques, motivational skills, career information, goal setting, decision making, etc. is required for all students in this program. This course is taught by the academic counselors.

All students are required to pass the required standardized and/or departmental test before receiving a grade for a DEP course.

E. Counseling Component

Each student is assigned to an academic counselor and is required to participate in individual and group sessions with the counselor. Active dialogue, especially regarding the student's involvement in the developmental education program, is encouraged. Counselors assist students in adjusting to academic and social pressures. A special component of counseling is direct intervention by the counselor in an effort to resolve problems of students and assist students in adjusting to academic and social pressures.

F. Tutorial Laboratory Instruction

Each student in the Developmental Education Program is required to attend the scheduled laboratory sessions designed to supplement the classroom instruction and to provide the needed practice work. Peer tutors (junior, senior, and graduate students) work with students on areas of deficiency. Faculty tutoring conference periods are scheduled in the Reading, Writing and Mathematics laboratories for teachers of those courses in addition to the use of classroom and office conferences.

Assessment, Placement and Exit Criteria Assessment

The American College Testing (ACT) Program is used for initial assessment of academic proficiency of students entering GSU for the first time. Each student admitted to GSU is asked to supply an ACT score or submit to ACT testing upon arrival. Students whose composite score on the ACT is fifteen or less are automatically scheduled by the counseling component of the Division of Academic Support Services into one of several levels of developmental English, reading and/or mathematics, depending on their math and/or English scores on the ACT.

Within two weeks of this placement, the student is given diagnostic tests in English, mathematics and reading to determine proper placement. For

English, the California Achievement Test (CAT), Form E, levels 19 and 20 (vocabulary, spelling, language mechanics, and language expression) is used. For mathematics, the Basic Algebra Test (of the Placement Test Program) of the Mathematical Association of America is used. The comprehension section of the Nelson-Denny Test is used to determine in which of the two reading groups to place students. An additional test, The Iowa Test of Basic Skills, Form 7, level 14 (comprehension, vocabulary, and reference) is administered for diagnostic purposes.

Placement

The placement of students into the various levels of English, mathematics and reading is determined by their score on the above placement tests. The range of scores and the course levels are indicated in the adjoining column.

Reading

We select 20 to 25 students to enroll in each Developmental Reading class. Students who score 8.9 and below in total reading proficiency on Nelson-Denny tests are placed in Developmental Reading 094. Students who score between 9.0 - 12.0 in total reading proficiency on Nelson-Denny test will be placed in Developmental Reading 095.

English

We select for enrollment in Developmental English 091 freshmen students whose ACT English scores are 15 or below and whose other diagnostic testing reveals a communicative skills competency at or below 9.9 grade level. We select for enrollment in Developmental English (English 092) freshman students whose ACT English scores are 15 or below and whose other diagnostic testing reveals a communicative skills competency between 10.0 and 11.4 grade levels. We select for enrollment in Developmental English (English 093) freshman students whose ACT English scores are 15 or below and whose other diagnostic testing reveals a communicative skills competency below 12.9 level.

Mathematics

Freshman students whose ACT Mathematics scores are less than 16 and whose other diagnostic mathematics scores show a competency grade equivalent of less than 9.0 are placed in Mathematics 096; those with competency grade equivalents of between 9.1 and 11.4 are placed in Math 097; those with competency grade equivalent scores of between 11.5 and 12.9 are placed in Math 098.

Placement of students in reading, Developmental English, and mathematics is shown in the following chart:

Course	Test Score (GE Score)
Reading	
Basic Reading 094	0.0 to 8.9
Basic Reading 095	9.0 to 12.0
English	
Basic English 091	0.0 to 9.9
Basic English 092	10.0 to 11.4
Basic English 093	11.5 to 12.9
Mathematics	
Basic Math 096	0.0 to 9.0
Basic Math 097	9.1 to 11.4
Basic Math 098	11.5 to 12.9

(NOTE: GE = GRADE EQUIVALENT)

Exit Criteria

In order to exit from a specific course or from the Developmental Education Program, a student must not only score significantly above the indicated ranges, but must also pass a departmental competency exam which includes writing skills, study skills, and library skills.

V. Training of Faculty, Counselors, Tutors

Meetings on a regular basis are used to discern and meet the training needs of program personnel. Each staff person is required to participate in extensive pre-service and in-service sessions.

VI. Program/Student Expectations

To insure that a program is truly developmental, certain requirements regarding the students and their participation in the program are defined.

Program emphasis is on progression. Students in the program are not labeled as disadvantaged, but as developmental, which reflects the progression expected through the program and the integrity within the university student body.

Course and program requirements are clear. Students are aware of expectations in various courses as well as those for college success. Each student is to develop to his other full potential with only high quality work being acceptable.

Retention in program components is essential. Drops from remedial courses are not allowed without extenuating circumstances. If a need exists to lessen the course load, other courses are dropped prior to remedial courses. By not allowing the student to leave the lower division until all needed remedial courses are complete, we build incentive toward early completion.

Guidance on a continual basis in developmental education is needed. Students are encouraged to review their own goals, commitments, and attitudes. They are carefully guided into realistic career choices and are permitted to make their own decisions.

Personal, social, and academic activities are reviewed in counseling and there's help in restructuring facets that are undesirable. Participation in various university activities is encouraged for acclimation to college.

Following their exit from the developmental education program students are carefully observed to determine additional counseling needs for one or two semesters.

VIII. Evaluation

Overall evaluation of the program, a component evaluation, faculty and counselor evaluation, and an evaluation of each student enrolled in the program is periodically conducted. Specific performance evaluation measurements are established for each component. The STEP Test is administered at the beginning of the fall semester to all students and again near the end of the spring semester to measure the progress over the nine-month session.

Accurate data is available to determine the progress of each student in the program and to determine the number and percentage of students who eventually graduate.

Specific performance evaluation measures are established and each student is required to meet established criteria to exit the program. Each student is required to meet the assigned academic counselor to discuss his or her performance and to determine if this program is beneficial to the student. Decisions are made with each student and his/her counselor after extensive testing to determine if college is a realistic choice and if not, each is given assistance in deciding on some other type of postsecondary training as required.

An extraordinary support feature of the Grambling State University Developmental Education Program is the fact that the program serves as the university's on-site laboratory for research and practicum for three graduate programs in developmental education, including the only doctoral degree in the field in the United States of America. Changes and modifications are made in the programs whenever necessary and justified. Such changes are subject to the approval of the Vice President for Academic Affairs and Research.

Special Services for Professional Students: Factors to Consider

ABOUT THE AUTHOR:

Dr. F. Marvin Hannah, Sr.

Dr. Hannah is the Director of Minority Affairs and Assistant to the Dean at Marquette University School of Dentistry. Prior to that appointment, he was a research associate at Waukesha County Technical College in Pewaukee, Wisconsin. He was also Program Director for the Metropolitan Milwaukee YMCA from 1983 to 1985, and Director of Minority Affairs at the Medical College of Wisconsin in Milwaukee from 1974-1981.

Dr. Hannah received a Ph.D. in Urban Social Institutions, M.S. in Urban Affairs, and B.S. in Social Welfare from the University of Wisconsin-Milwaukee. He has acted as chair of committees in education and community services, and consultant to schools and colleges. Dr. Hannah is a co-founder of Wisconsin Affirmative Action and Equal Opportunity Professionals, and has served as both President and Vice-President of that organization.

INTRODUCTION

Few non-whites are entering into the preparation and training for careers in health, law, engineering, architecture, accounting, and other professions. The attrition rate for non-whites who do enroll in professional schools is higher than the attrition rate for white students. Two of the reasons for the higher attrition rate are related to non-white students' academic preparation for professional studies, and a lack of concern about their retention. To remedy and address these factors it is important for professional schools to implement support activities prior to students' enrollment, and for the academic support system to support and enhance their retention once enrolled. Professional schools that are pro-active rather than reactive to these issues will experience greater non-white student retention and graduation rates.

SPECIAL SERVICES FOR PROFESSIONAL STUDENTS:

Factors to
Consider

by
F. Marvin
Hannah, Sr., Ph.D.

In the early 1970s many U.S. colleges and universities initiated a variety of program models to identify, motivate, prepare, recruit, enroll, retain and graduate non-white students at the graduate and professional school levels. Non-whites are defined as African-Americans, Asian-Americans, Mexican-Americans, mainland Puerto Ricans, American Indians, Eskimos and Aluets. Historically, the proportion of non-whites in health care, engineering, accounting, law, and other professions has always been less than the ratio of non-whites in the general population. Decades of segregation and discrimination have resulted in unequal educational opportunity, including a relative lack of access to education in the professions. The result is a gross underrepresentation of non-white professionals among the total number of practicing professionals in America.

The shortage of minority professionals exists despite the fact that the number of non-white students entering professional schools increased during the 1970s. The narrowing of the gap necessary to attain parity has been impeded by a slow-down in the increases of the number of new non-white professional students since the mid-1980s (Black Issues in Higher Education, 1989).

During the 1990s efforts must be undertaken to motivate youth to prepare for a professional career. For those non-whites already in the educational pipeline and about to enter professional studies, there are factors which can inhibit their academic progress and success. This article discusses several factors concerned with the matriculation and retention of the non-white professional student. The opinions expressed are based on my seven years experience as Director of Minority Affairs for the Medical College of Wisconsin, a private medical school located in Milwaukee, Wisconsin, and my three years as Director of Minority Affairs and Assistant to the Dean at Marquette University School of Dentistry, a private Jesuit university, also located in Milwaukee. Although references are made to professional education and training, most of the examples cited are to the medical and dental professions.

Minority Affairs Personnel in Professional School

Most professional schools have established Minority Student Affairs offices. These offices are charged with designing, organizing, and administering academic support programs to identify, recruit, admit, and retain non-white students. It is important that minority affairs offices are staffed with professionals who are culturally sensitive to the students with whom they work. This is key because of the cultural dynamics which are often at play in non-white student relations and affairs.

Often what non-white minority affairs professionals seek to accomplish is in conflict with other interests in the school. However, minority affairs personnel must aggressively address those concerns that do and can affect the academic progress of non-white students. Minority affairs professionals have viewed themselves as "gatekeepers," protecting the interests (i.e., graduation) of the non-white professional student.

Racism in Professional Education

One would expect the atmosphere and individuals at the professional education level to be mature, tolerant, and concerned only with the art and science of the professional discipline. This is not the case. Racism is a world order and non-white students enrolled in white professional schools will experience some form of racism during their professional education experience. I state this without fear of equivocation or contradiction. Some white student, faculty member, or staff person will through ignorance, fear, jealousy, or purposeful intent say or do something to remind the non-white student of his/her racial or ethnic difference. Despite efforts to encourage and establish positive race relations in professional schools, bigotry and prejudicial remarks are still present, victimizing non-white students.

To a large extent, race relations in professional education depend on top administrators' demonstrated commitment to cultural diversity. Each administration, through its policies and actions, sets the stage for race relations to flourish or to languish within the professional school environment. One way towards achieving good race relations is successful recruitment of non-white faculty and staff. Racist behavior is reduced when an institution has non-white faculty and staff. One method for recruiting non-white faculty, given the current non-white faculty pool, is for an institution to hire its own graduates or arrange with other professional schools to exchange non-white graduates as faculty.

To deny the existence of racial conflict in a culturally diverse student population is folly. Professional school administrators must be willing to facilitate open discussion on race relations when problems do occur. Openness contributes to reducing racial conflict and can lead to solutions.

I instruct non-white students on how to deal with racism. Students need not accept racist behavior and discriminatory practices directed against them. Minority Affairs and other university personnel can inform students how to effectively address racial issues and assist them in following through when appropriate. This can be accomplished with student seminars at the beginning of each year for the incoming class. I invite key administrators to such seminars to address students on relevant topics.

Pre-Matriculation Concerns

Helping the non-white student before he or she arrives at the professional school has positive short and long term retention effects. I recommend sending non-white students information prior to arrival on campus. A new student orientation for non-white students just before the start of classes is also suggested. Both activities give the non-white student a head start in settling in and down prior to starting classes. The student is able to complete many non-academic tasks before classes begin and thus can concentrate solely on course work when classes do begin. A good start is very important. Students who get behind at the beginning have difficulty catching up with their academic work.

Minority Affairs professionals should consider designing a student handbook. School policies, procedures, and guidelines should be covered. Community and institutional services for non-white students can be included. For example, information about local churches, and family and community services catering to non-whites would help many students. The handbook could contain such information as where an African-American male can get a haircut, an African-American female a beauty salon treatment, where the Puerto Rican student can purchase plantain, or the Mexican-American student atole, frijoles or mole, and the location of the American Indian cultural center. This handbook should address the personal or academic concerns the more traditional student handbooks may not consider important, but the knowledge of which will make life more enjoyable for the non-white student.

Enrolling in a professional school is an anxious, stressful time for any student. Non-white students often enter the professional education experience doubtful as to whether they will even survive academically until the next semester. They often feel added psychological pressure that a personal failure would disappoint "the race." The white professional student does not have such pressure. For some non-white students this type of pressure can be positive reinforcement, but for others it can negatively affect their academic success. Minority Affairs professionals need to be aware of this type of stress and how to identify and counter its impact.

Helping Non-white Students Succeed in School

Since the mid 1970s, attempts to provide pre-professional non-white students with missing academic foundations have been offered primarily through undergraduate pre-entry programs, summer enrichment activity, or post-baccalaureate program models. These programs are aimed at retaining non-white students and enhancing their academic performances and quality of studies (Cadbury, 1979).

In general, summer enrichment programs inform and introduce non-white undergraduate students to the practical and simulated experiences associated with the pursuit of a professional career, providing students with a more realistic approach to the requirements for entrance into professional careers (Cadbury, 1979).

Post-baccalaureate and summer pre-enrollment programs provide a "bridge" between under-graduate and professional studies. These programs increase non-white students' ability to successfully compete in the professional education curriculum. They enrich students' knowledge of the rigors of the professional education courses, improve study skills, diagnose academic strengths and weaknesses, reinforce motivation for the career, and in general help promote academic success and retention. Pre-enrollment programs that terminate just prior to the start of classes enable students to "hit the ground running," highly motivated and confident of their own abilities to successfully compete with classmates.

Early Intervention: Factors to Consider

Non-white student academic problems may or may not stem from their difficulty in understanding or completing course materials. Academic difficulties may be the result of a personal problem that negatively affects academic work. Whatever the basis for a student's lack of academic achievement or failure to keep abreast of their professional studies, the chief concern is to discover (or uncover) the problem early and act decisively.

Early intervention cannot be overstated. Intervention strategies when implemented early can keep the problem from overwhelming the student. Since the faculty are initially the individuals most likely to discover any changes in the students' demeanor, attitude, and academic progress, they must be a part of any early intervention strategy.

The faculty can be the first to alert those responsible for the retention of non-white students of any problem or change. Once a problem has been identified, the appropriate remedial or academic support should be quickly implemented. It may be difficult to motivate the non-white professional student to attend remedial or tutorial sessions (pride, denial, etc.), but institutional sanctions and rewards should not be overlooked to obtain compliance.

An "Academic Alert System" I developed for dental students incorporates the above mechanism and has demonstrated its effectiveness in bringing institutional and community resources to address students problems. Every student brought to the attention of the Minority Affairs Office through the "Alert" system has been helped without delay. When it was determined tutorial assistance was needed, a tutor was assigned; when it was determined a student needed personal assistance for themselves or their family, the office was able to address the issue.

The Minority Affairs professional (or others) has to identify resources ahead of time so that when assistance is needed it can quickly be obtained. Community services and resources (non-white when appropriate and available) include but are not limited to religious and psychological services, welfare and human services, child care, employment, medical, dental, and legal assistance.

Non-white professional students can also be a source of support and assistance for one another through peer counseling programs. Upper-class students can counsel their junior colleagues on the who, what, when, where, and how of completing professional education. Students sometimes find it easier to talk to other non-white students about some things. Peer counseling can include the student's spouse and family. These activities can aid students' psychological, social and emotional stability and thus enhance retention.

Retention Factors

Student retention services have to be pro-active rather than reactive. Not all non-white students enrolled in a professional school will need academic assistance; however, academic support should be in place to help students in a timely manner.

I suggest mandatory study skills seminars for new students during the first week of classes. The seminars should include diagnosis of acquired skills, and should be taught by skilled, trained professionals in the areas of study skills, time management, note taking, problem solving, using library and institution resources and test taking techniques.

Professional schools with non-native speaking non-white students should provide audio-visual resources and English as second language courses to improve their English proficiency. Pairing non-native English speaking students in study groups and laboratory sessions with native speakers should also be considered.

The Decelerated Curriculum as a Retention Strategy

In general, the decelerated curriculum extends the professional educational curriculum beyond its usual length of time. For example, a four-year curriculum may be extended to five years. The purpose is to provide the student with a reduced academic load at a slower pace to help him or her meet curricula standards.

Some professional schools automatically enroll non-white students in a decelerated curriculum upon their admission. Others allow a six-to eight-week trial period at the beginning of the first year to allow students to demonstrate appropriate placement in a decelerated curriculum. However, to assume that all non-white students need a decelerated curriculum is an error.

Test Taking

The non-white student can often fail courses because of an inability to successfully take or complete tests. That is why instruction to improve test taking skills and techniques is important. Allowing additional time for non-white students to take examinations is a retention strategy to be considered. No valid educational canon is violated when students are given 80 or 90 minutes to complete a traditional hour long exam, especially when it is known the student will achieve a passing score if given the additional time. Professional schools should review their policies regarding examination time lengths and when possible allow additional time. This simple policy change can make a tremendous difference in non-white students' retention rates.

Finally, Consider This

The professional education process should include opportunities for the student to be exposed to and tutored by a practicing non-white professional. These interactions can aid the student's maturity and character. Such interactions can be incorporated in the curriculum, or offered as an extracurricular activity.

Non-white professional students can likewise act as mentors for non-white pre-professional students. Tutoring activities at this level involve giving advice, and providing counsel and assistance in preparing for admission into professional studies. In a larger community, a formative level of interaction should begin at the elementary level to inform young non-white persons about various professional opportunities. The professional student can serve as a role model, advising non-white elementary students to begin thinking about the more rigorous academic courses in the future.

Consider this: If the practicing non-white professional were to nurture and encourage just one non-white professional student to graduation, and if the non-white professional student were to do the same with young people to admission into professional studies, the problem of non-white underrepresentation in professional disciplines would be greatly reduced and the nation better off because of the efforts.

References

Cadbury, William E., and Cadbury, Charlotte, M. (1979). *Medical Education: Responses to a Challenge.* Mount Kisco, New York: Futura Publishing Company.

Hannah, Frederick, M., Sr. (1988). *The Junior Academy of Medicine: A Case Study of a Preparatory Program for the Discipline.* Diss. University of Wisconsin-Milwaukee.

Report, (1989). *The Declining Enrollment of Minority Graduate Students: Trends, Problems, Issues, Solutions.* Black Issues in Higher Education, 6, June 8.

Upward Bound Programs
Why they Succeed with Minority Students

ABOUT THE AUTHOR:

Deltha Q.
Colvin

Deltha Q. Colvin is the Assistant Dean of Students and Director of the Upward Bound Program at The Wichita State University in Wichita, Kansas. She also serves as the TRIO Coordinator for the Student Support Services and Talent Search Programs. Colvin, a former Upward Bound student herself, has been involved with TRIO Programs since 1965. She earned her B. A. from Wichita State University and has earned 36 post-graduate hours in education there also.

Colvin is also a trainer and consultant in all aspects of the administration of TRIO Programs (Special Services Programs funded by the Department of Education) and works with minority and disadvantaged students. She has served in leadership roles at the regional and national level in the TRIO Associations. Committed to equal access and opportunity for minority and disadvantaged students, she remains active on the national level in TRIO affairs.

INTRODUCTION

Research has shown that pre-school programs help kids throughout life. Studies have found that youngsters who attended pre-school had higher employment, high school and college graduation rates, performed better on tests, were in less trouble with the law and in general contributed more to society. It often takes targeted efforts to get Minority students thinking about college at an early age. It should be kept in mind that college has not been a "family experience" for most minority students.

A pre-college program can be to campuses what Head Start programs are to elementary schools. Both programs are designed to prepare students for a successful schooling experience. They assess students' academic weaknesses and strengths and provide assistance to overcome deficiencies.

Perhaps the most successful pre-collegiate programs are Upward Bound programs, in which middle and high school students actually live on campus, take college courses, and interact with faculty. Upward Bound programs have been extremely effective in motivating "disadvantaged" high school students to attend and graduate from college.

In this article the Upward Bound program, its history, funding, and goals are described. The operation of the program, the types of students involved, the summer and school-year components, and Saturday Sessions are detailed. Each description is accompanied by a practical justification for the existence of that practice or component.

Over 800,000 students have graduated from Upward Bound programs over the past twenty-four years and now have successful careers because a group of dedicated personnel saw their potential and invested in students' futures.

Upward Bound Programs:

Why they Succeed with Minority Students

by
Deltha Q.
Colvin

The Upward Bound program is a pre-college program. It was first established in 1964 under authority provided by the Economic Opportunities Act. This program was designed to generate (1) the academic skill, and (2) the necessary motivation to prepare low-income, underachieving students for success in education beyond high school.

To receive funding for an Upward Bound program, accredited colleges and universities and, in exceptional cases, secondary schools, submit project proposals outlining their plans to enhance the academic preparation and to improve the motivation of Upward Bound students by means of programs which can include remedial instruction, altered curricula, tutoring, cultural exposure and encouragement so that the students can succeed in higher education.

Although the program is designed to help students who have completed the eighth grade and are at least thirteen years old, the Department of Education considers proposals to help students who are less than thirteen or have not completed the 8th grade when student dropout rates at such schools are unusually high. In contrast, the Department of Education guidelines discourage the recruiting of students who have entered the twelfth grade, because they would be enrolled in the program for only one summer, indicating that this would be too brief a period to allow adequate time for the project to provide the services and assistance needed in preparation for post-secondary education.

A typical Upward Bound project includes a summer and an academic year component. The summer component is a six to eight week residential program on a college, university, or secondary school campus where the students are provided academic and cultural enrichment classes, tutoring sessions, and academic and personal counseling. The primary purpose of the academic year component is to maintain the gains made during the intensive summer session. During the academic year, each student's high school class schedule is developed with a high school counselor and a member of the Upward Bound staff to insure that students follow a college preparatory curriculum. Professional staff members from the Upward Bound project continue to maintain contact with the participants by means of Saturday classes, tutorials, career workshops, counseling sessions, and periodic cultural enrichment activities.

A typical Upward Bound project works with a predetermined number of junior or senior high school students. Each project has a full-time professional staff which usually consists of a project director, one or more counselors, an academic coordinator, clerical/technical assistance and in some instances, tutors and peer counselors. The primary objective of this staff is to provide programs and services designed to encourage student participation in the learning environment.

Throughout the summer and academic year components, the following programs and services are provided year round:

1. Instruction in reading, writing, study skills, mathematics, and other subjects necessary for success in education beyond high school;

2. Personal counseling;

3. Academic advice and assistance in high school course selection;

4. Tutorial services;

5. Exposure to cultural events, academic programs, and other activities not usually available to disadvantaged youth;

6. Activities designed to acquaint youths participating in the project with the range of career options available to them;

7. Instruction designed to prepare youths participating in the project for careers in which persons from disadvantaged backgrounds are particularly underrepresented;

8. On-campus residential programs; and

9. Programs and activities specifically designed for individuals with limited proficiency in English.

For an Upward Bound program to be successful, it must have a comprehensive management plan. That management plan must include an academic year component, tutorial services, Saturday sessions and a summer component. Each of these units will be discussed in this article.

Programs are structured to prepare each participant to make a successful transition from secondary to post-secondary education. Minority students are given one-on-one attention and consistency that is generally not available to them. The projects ensure equal educational opportunity.

All students need a support system of individuals who care and are willing to go the extra mile to ensure opportunities for their success. Upward Bound provides such a network for these students. A student must begin to accept the responsibility for his or her own education and the planning for a career. Minority students have the opportunity to establish an educational support group which provides direction, instruction and cultural exposure. Upward Bound provides opportunity for skills enhancement and acquisition of new skills. The staff believes in the student's potential for post-secondary success.

Activities and services are planned to move a student through each year of high school. Classes, academic performance, skills, aptitudes and motivation are monitored monthly. For the minority student this allows for intervention to implement strategies to correct problems. One-on-one and group tutoring and counseling affords the staff an opportunity to provide positive feedback and support to address problems. Each situation is handled to provide the best assistance to meet the needs of the individual student. Assistance may include referrals, post-secondary planning, academic course work, and skills improvement.

Academic skills and the motivational level of participants are key factors in the student's development and success in education beyond high school. The project's academic and summer activities are generally designed to assist in providing basic and advanced academic skills. Academic course work taken during the academic year is important because grades earned are counted toward graduation and post-secondary preparation. The project's services strengthen the likelihood of good grades, motivation, and success after high school.

Academic Year Component

The *Academic Year Component* is designed to maintain positive contact with participants, augment basic skills instruction, provide supportive services in counseling and tutoring, assist with post-secondary preparation and continue exposure to cultural/social events.

The curriculum is developed in cooperation with the school system to assure continuity. Students receive instruction in school-required course work; every effort is made to prevent confusion. Classes are often taught by certified public school teachers or graduate students. Services provided to students can include instruction, tutoring, sessions on test and note taking, study skills, and career development. Seminars concerning careers underrepresented by minorities, handicapped and women, and visits to local agencies and post-secondary institutions, are conducted. Individual and group tutoring and counseling sessions held weekly provide students consistency and stability, enhancing the likelihood of success.

A student's project schedule is designed to foster full participation in academic and non-academic activities offered by the secondary school. Tutorial sessions are arranged to afford students the maximum benefit from both school and Upward Bound. Project sessions can be scheduled to allow students participating in school athletics an opportunity for involvement in scheduled practice sessions. Students are encouraged and prepared for participation in school events. For a minority student elected to an Upward Bound student council position, it's possible to see the chances of being elected in school. Risks taken in Upward Bound provide motivation for interest in school events. Peers and staff support a student's interests and efforts. Students can improve their chances of being successful in areas where they have feared taking chances, and they see the value of involving themselves in activities.

The *Academic Year Component* allows the project to strengthen the educational/career skills development that affects educational/career aspirations after high school.

A relationship is established with school counselors, community agencies, and other resource persons to ensure referral contacts to assistance students. These sources are used to make referrals needed for counseling, special testing and motivation. Referrals are important because minority students see that individuals beyond those in the school system and Upward Bound are interested in their welfare. Often assistance is provided free or for a minimal charge. This assistance helps the student and the family.

Monitoring participants' academic growth enables staff working with students to aid their progress. Through written progress reports, which obtain information on student attendance, grades, motivation, skills, attention span, classroom participation, attitude, sincerity, tardiness, completion of assignments, college preparation, cooperation and confidence development, the ability to work with others and the need for tutorial support, the staff can assist students with strategies to make improvements. Progress reports allow the Upward Bound staff and students to implement strategies to insure course work is completed, attendance improved, basic skills strengthened, and grades improved. Meetings can be held with the student, where they may be provided with a copy of the analysis and needed improvements. These sessions will give staff indications of how the student plans to improve. Meetings and reports provide regularly scheduled assessments and progress in the students' development. Tutors working with students can refer to these records to emphasize special areas of concentration and assess what assignments and skills should be covered during tutorial sessions.

Assessments are used to ascertain the strengths and weaknesses in a student's skills. Staff can prepare the participant for standardized assessments. Through practice sessions, students can be prepared for college entrance exams, improve academic weaknesses, and acquire test taking techniques to reduce their level of anxiety. The importance of preparation for assessments and their impact on post-secondary entrance is stressed to participants.

Academic instruction and workshops are set up for students to increase skills and provide information that encourages academic and social advancement.

Tutorial Sessions

Tutoring is done in groups or one-on-one. One-on-one tutoring is beneficial for several reasons:

1. To avoid duplicating the classroom setting that the student experiences;

2. There are fewer distractions and less socializing which can interfere with studying;

3. The student receives the help needed because the tutor's attention is not divided among several students;

4. Individual tutoring increases the student's sense of self-worth and importance because the tutor is available for that student; and

5. Concentration is given to the specific needs and learning style of the student.

The success of a tutoring program depends on the effort and commitment of the student and tutor. The tutor and student must be committed to attending tutorial sessions regularly. Students must be interested in receiving assistance to better understand the course work and not in having the tutor do the work for them. Understanding a subject is more important than memorizing information to get a grade. Students are assisted with under-standing and learning rules, formulas, theories and techniques to advance to more complex subjects. Tutors participate in training sessions to ensure they are aware of techniques that would ensure their understanding of different learning styles. Tutorial sessions teach students and tutors a sense of personal responsibility and consideration of others.

Saturday Sessions

Upward Bound *Saturday Sessions* are designed to maintain contact with the participants, provide tutorial assistance, expose students to career options, provide instruction, expose students to cultural enrichment, and assist with personal and academic counseling. Programs will provide any combination of these areas to ensure students maintain an ongoing support system. Minority students often do not receive this type of regulated, consistent exposure. These areas augment the student's general activities and ensure access to support systems when problems arise that affect academic and social performance. Students' personal problems that conflict with their progress in school and tutorial sessions are discussed with staff who are willing to listen to the students' problems and concerns and give unbiased opinions.

Graduating students are provided extensive individualized and group counseling for post-secondary preparation. These students are provided financial aid, admissions and college planning sessions to acquaint them with the application process. Students are informed of national deadlines and required assessments, and are provided with technical assistance to complete paper work. Upward Bound staff members train students to complete the paper work themselves to ensure they can complete financial aid and other forms on their own while attending a post-secondary institution. Upward Bound emphasizes the need to be independent to succeed in school. Parents are asked to attend post-secondary planning sessions with their child to encourage support and awareness of the requirements for continued receipt of financial assistance. College planning sessions help minority students overcome some of the barriers that present obstacles to a post-secondary education. A clear presentation of requirements ensures the likelihood for post-secondary success.

Upward Bound projects seek to provide activities of an enrichment nature, which may be fun, to enhance the students' social and emotional growth. Some of these activities are a first time experience for students. They may include camping, skiing, bowling, concerts, theatrical productions, museum visits, historical sites, Indian pow-wows, Mexican fiestas, and Black arts festivals and celebrations. Cultural Enrichment Activities provide cultural exposure and pride, self-esteem, and general exposure to the larger society. Cultural pride can stimulate motivation in all aspects of the student's life. The student becomes more involved, is motivated to perform well academically and wants to make a contribution. Minority students can see others like themselves who are successful and aspiring to reach their goals. They are also exposed to activities in which minorities are underrepresented. Staff are aware of the responsibility to prepare future leaders. Research on the nation's demographics shows that minority students will be the majority in classrooms in the twenty-first century.

Summer Component

The purpose of the *Summer Residential Component* is to provide academic instruction, tutoring, guidance and counseling (individual and group), career information, advising and assistance, post-secondary classes, and exposure to cultural events and daily academic programs. All activities are designed to stimulate a college-going experience for participants. Students are in residence from 6-8 weeks. The residential and academic experience exposes the student to the atmosphere they would experience in college. During the 6-8 week summer program the staff provides structured, daily assistance to students. It is an opportunity to expose participants to college life.

The opportunity to be on the campus, walk among and interact with college students and faculty, receive daily attention with academic and social development and establish a multicultural peer network, prepares students for the college experience. Students participate in an infrastructure that is conducive to learning, study, skills enhancement, personal development and motivation for education. Participants are taught more than academics; knowledge of good eating habits, how they fit into the larger society, race relations, where to go and who to contact when personal problems arise, and the abundance of social options available to them are also stressed. The program provides a well rounded exposure to academic development and life.

For some students, this infrastructure is their first exposure to a regimented environment designed to address their needs and concerns. Furthermore, it is an opportunity for the exploration of career options they've dreamed about or seriously considered. A professional and paraprofessional staff serve as role models students can confide in and utilize to assist with skills enhancement. The staff, therefore, have the opportunity to become familiar with each student and his or her own needs.

Some programs conclude their summer with an academic and enrichment trip for participants who successfully complete the summer program. This exposes students to environments outside of their area. Many students rarely travel outside of their city or home state. The summer trip and academic campus visits provide glimpses of the larger society, options open to them, role models like them, and the reality that minorities are making gains.

For projects giving high school credit for summer classes, it gives the student who received a poor grade an opportunity to improve the grade. This keeps the student on track with his or her graduating class and affords him or her special attention to ensure success.

The intense *Summer Residential Program* promotes academic and social growth in a setting conducive to educational advancement. The staff has a captive audience that has an interest in honing skills, has academic potential, and is considering post-secondary education. Activities provide exposure to all aspects of their development.

Conclusion

Upward Bound is a pre-college program that provides many opportunities to students. The structure of the program is conducive to motivating participants to take the program and their academic development seriously, take advantage of opportunities, and prepare for education beyond high school. Services provided by a project can assist the student if the student is willing to do the work. Over eight hundred thousand students have graduated from Upward Bound Programs over the past twenty-four years and have successful careers because a group of dedicated personnel saw their potential and invested in the students' future. The students believed they could accomplish their goals and made the commitment to strengthen their skills. Students are provided equal access and opportunity for a post-secondary education with the help of this project.

The exposure, skills learned and personal development will impact the students' lives whether they complete college or pursue another course. The information and skills acquired may pave the way for a student to settle on a specialized vocational career or the military. Important is the fact that the student is a more productive and informed member of the larger society. Further, they are a living success story, as are TRIO Achievers who motivate and encourage other students to aspire to educational excellence. Much of the impact made by the program may not be realized by the student until many years after participation, but the experiences in the program will be a part of the student's past and present. The Upward Bound staff realized through visits of returning students that they gained and acquired many skills that were not apparent to them during participation.

Minority students are provided the one-on-one and specialized attention necessary to improve their academic skills and social development. They have been assisted with the resources and preparation to advance toward their goal and dreams. Participants are made aware of the types of resources available on a college campus, along with the Student Support Services Program (another TRIO program) that can further assist them. Students are encouraged to be assertive and take advantage of all opportunities available to them. Upward Bound encourages minority participants to graduate from high school with the skills to pursue post-secondary education and matriculate toward a degree. A student participating for three to four years would have received college preparation, basic skills development, cultural exposure, personal development, academic discipline, and the motivation to be the first in their immediate or extended family to receive a post-secondary degree. Students receive positive and supportive reinforcement from staff; students gain self-confidence and set long-term goals. Minority students are given a chance to beat the odds.

Application of Cognitive Therapy
for African-American Female Athletes

ABOUT THE AUTHOR:

Mary
Howard-Hamilton

Mary Howard-Hamilton is a doctoral student in the Department of Counselor Education at North Carolina State University, and is the Assistant Area Director for the Department of Housing and Residence Life at the E.S. King Village Family/ Student Housing Complex.

She formerly served as the Associate Dean of Students at the University of North Carolina at Charlotte, where she was the first recipient of an award in her name given to an outstanding faculty member or administrator. She also served as Assistant Dean of Students at Coe College in Cedar Rapids, Iowa.

Ms. Howard-Hamilton received her M.A. in College Student Personnel Administration from the University of Iowa in 1977 and received her B.A. in Speech and Dramatic Arts from that same university in 1976. Ms. Howard-Hamilton has worked closely with numerous student groups, particularly African-American and non-traditional scholars. She has presented workshops at numerous conferences on topics pertaining to minority student retention, orientation programming, Greek life, leadership strategies, and racism. As an academic scholar, Mary is focusing her research on issues related to fear of success and the gifted adolescent female, peer mentoring, African-American student development, and the socialization process of African-American females.

INTRODUCTION

The African-American female athlete must overcome many obstacles before, during and after her collegiate career. There have been relatively few researchers exploring the developmental issues as they relate to female college athletes and, more specifically, the issues of racism, sexism, and socialization of the African-American female athlete.

The author's study contributes to the literature by naming the psychosocial and social cognition of the African-American female athlete, and how her cognitive development and issues of socialization impact future career consideration.

Strategies are provided that counselors and therapists can implement to help the African-American female athlete become more self-efficacious in her career decision-making skills.

APPLICATION OF COGNITIVE THERAPY

for African-American
Female Athletes

by
Mary
Howard-Hamilton

African-American female athletes must overcome tremendous psychological, identity and cultural barriers in order to succeed on a predominantly white campus. Green, Olglesby, Alexander and Franke (1981) noted that "to become a fine athlete she has to develop an assessment of herself in the face of society which devalues her, as both a female and a Black" (p. 1).

Personality and self-concept development begins early in childhood. Self-concept and identity is shaped by one's assessment of how others view and feel about oneself (Exum, 1986; Powell, 1979). A child is guided by external factors such as social groups, physical attributes; group norms, achievement, and aspirations (Powell, 1979). It is important, therefore, that the young African-American female be encouraged and receive healthy social and emotional support so she may develop a positive self-concept. Future career aspirations are based upon how the African-American female is able to cope with her "differences;" a firm identity-formation and realistic life plans depend upon completion of her athletic/academic pursuits.

The purpose of this paper is to offer a deliberate psychological education program to African American female college athletes. It also presents a carefully structured program designed to promote, not assume development.

Socialization of the Female Athlete

A review of the literature revealed that the family is the primary initiator of females into sport activities (Ames, 1984; Green et al., 1981; Greendorfer, 1987; Greendorfer, 1983; Higginson, 1985; Sapiro, 1987). One cannot devalue the importance of the family role in sports because attitudes towards sports participation are included within family values, traditions, and customs that are perpetuated and passed on from generation to generation (Greendorfer, 1983).

Children are socialized by their parents and are exposed to activities consonant with their gender role (Greendorfer, 1983; Selby, 1989). Parents influence and nurture their child's sex-role formation by encouraging the son to emulate his father. Concomitantly, daughters are taught appropriate female activities by their mothers who serve as role models.

Children play with games, toys, or activities that society feels are appropriate for their sex (Greendorfer, 1983; Sage & Loudermilk, 1979; Selby, 1989). The types of toys purchased for boys and girls exemplify the sex-typing and differentiation society has placed upon sports and play. Further evidence why girls do not select sports activities or become athletes is also shown in the types of games children play (Sage & Loudermilk, 1979). Greendorfer (1983) stated that boys play games which facilitate teamwork, decision-making, and collaboration as part of their learning process. She also notes that girl's games do not have structural organization nor do they offer similar social learning outcomes.

Various types of athletic activity are perceived by girls as masculine and socially unacceptable or feminine and socially acceptable. For example, basketball, volleyball, and soccer would be considered masculine because each is a team sport and would involve bodily contact or touching one's opponents (Ames, 1984; Greendorfer, 1987; Greendorfer, 1983; Sage & Loudermilk, 1979). However, figure skating, gymnastics and synchronized swimming emphasize grace, skill and beauty, and are therefore socially acceptable for women's competition (Greendorfer, 1983; Sage & Loudermilk, 1979). As noted by Edwards (1973), it is considered appropriate for women to participate in sports where a physical barrier separates opponents, and activities which involve grace and aesthetically pleasing movements are preferred. He also stated that while males are participating in

football, basketball, baseball, boxing and wrestling; women are propelling themselves gracefully over the ice or through the water, or slapping the ball over a tennis net.

The media has a propensity to perpetuate these stereotypes. Halpert (1988) observed that:

> We see on our screens amazing feats of female strength, speed, and endurance. Yet there's a persistent buzz to suggest that this athleticism is somehow atypical; indeed, abnormal. At the opening of the women's downhill skiing competition in Calgary, as a montage of female athletes flashed on the screen, ABC's Al Trautwig chose to observe, "at some point these women were all normal little girls. Somewhere along the way they got sidetracked" (p. 36).

African-American Females and Sport

Edwards (1973) hypothesized that cultures where male and female roles are less sharply defined than dominant American society, or where these roles are reversed, should be more accepting of the female athlete.

Hanks (1979) suggested that female participation in athletic programs may be more socially acceptable in the African-American community than in the white community. A primary reason is that the African-American community may impose fewer limitations on sport involvement than the white community (Coakley, 1978). Also, athletic achievements are more important in the development of self-concept for African-Americans than for whites (Hanks, 1979). Hart (cited in Edwards, 1973) found that:

> there is a startling contrast between the Black and white female athlete. In the Black community it seems a woman can be strong and competent in sport and still not deny her "womanliness." She can even win respect and high status (p. 233).

Edwards (1973) asserted that a stellar African-American female athlete is celebrated as a champion in her own right. He also found that her athletic adeptness is neither evaluated in terms of male athletic accomplishments, nor is it perceived as detrimental to her femininity. Conversely, athletic ability by white female athletes is continually being evaluated by standards assigned by white men. The author also exclaimed,

> The more [their athletic ability] approximates those of males, the more the white females' "womanliness" becomes suspect (p. 234).

Due to financial constraints and socialization by defining activities as "upper" and "lower" class sports, African-American women have clustered themselves into two primary athletic arenas -- track and basketball (Green et al., 1981). These sports do not require extensive financial backing, equipment, or hiring of coaches ; but do allow access to public facilities and are built into school programs throughout the country (Green et al., 1981).

Several myths have emerged about African-American women in society and sport (Green et al., 1981, p. 56-57):

> Black women are better off than Black men because they can generally obtain employment;
>
> Black women have emasculated Black men;
>
> The Black society is matriarchal;
>
> Blacks cannot swim -- their bodily composition is too dense;
>
> Black females are more (sic) difficult to coach;
>
> Black women can only excel in track and field and basketball;
>
> The Black woman must be a superstar to make the team;
>
> Black females are not intelligent -- use them in positions that require speed and not brains;
>
> Blacks are lazy; and
>
> Black teams are excessively aggressive.

The constant resurgence of these myths is the common reason why Black women are not ardent participators in sports activities (Green et al., 1981).

The Campus Experience

An African-American female athlete has numerous obstacles hurled at her when attending a predominately white institution (Alexander, 1979; Gerdy, 1987):

> (1) She is considered a "dumb jock" like so many other athletes;
>
> (2) She is African-American and female which is the lowest cultural group in society's hierarchy of "approved" ethnic, racial, and sexual groups;
>
> (3) She experiences "culture shock" at the institution. This is primarily perpetuated by her lack of peer support, homesickness, stressful athletic/academic schedule, and lack of role models or professional mentors;
>
> (4) She experiences stress and depression due to the need to win, excel, and maintain the image society places on athletes as superstars.

In the academic community, the athlete is viewed as pampered and functionally distinct, a not very intelligent nor well-rounded individual (Gerdy, 1987).

A major concern is the African-American athletes' perception of self-worth and self-esteem as articulated by Alexander (1979):

> Athletes grow up with mixed messages about themselves, which often result in the individual being confused about his (sic) self-worth. When an athlete is repeatedly reinforced for his athletic performance, that individual begins to see his personal worth as tied inextricably to the athletic ability. Many of these individuals begin to experience feelings of ambivalence, resisting the belief that personal worth begins and ends with identifiable athletic ability, (p. 141).

As the African-American female athlete matriculates through school, which reaps the benefits of her talents for the length of her eligibility, when does she begin to prepare herself psychosocially and cognitively for her future endeavors?

Few white coaches attempt to get African-American athletes satisfactory summer jobs while they are eligible for sports; and no concerted effort will be put forth after the athletes' eligibility has expired (Edwards, 1970). The athlete is hopelessly and ultimately forced to be independent. Teresa Edwards, All-American basketball player from the University of Georgia stated that:

> as soon as the last ball started bouncing, I knew I was in the real world. I did not have anyone to tell me what to do or where to be (Budweiser Sports Report, 1989).

It is difficult for the African-American female athlete to gain fame or fortune from her athletic ability following her collegiate career. Halpert (1988) found the following:

> Ironically, some of the best remembered Olympians have been women: Olga Korbut, Nadia Comaneci, Dorothy Hamill and Mary Lou Retton. But their visibility was a by-product of media coverage that transforms the Games into the athletic equivalent of the Miss World beauty pageant. Every four years we have the crowning of a bright, enthusiastic girl; usually a pixie, always white, who has won hearts with her "spunky" performance and "winning smile" (p. 38).

What is left for the African-American female athlete to aspire to when her entire self-concept is based upon her athletic prowess? The career options available to her are limited. She could play overseas, complete her degree requirements, coach, or attempt to find some transferrable skill from basketball to the business world.

A cognitive social and developmental model can be used as a means for guiding the African-American female athlete through her psychosocial and career transition.

Cognitive Developmental Frameworks

Erik Erikson (cited in Sprinthall & Collins, 1988) developed a theoretical framework of psychosocial growth or identity development. He has been referred to as "the man who gave

adolescents identity crises" (Sprinthall & Collins, 1988, p. 145).

> Erikson's philosophy was that development continued throughout one's lifetime (Sprinthall & Sprinthall, 1987). Special significance was placed on childhood (birth to six years), the juvenile era (six to twelve years), and adolescence (twelve through the college years).

Erikson's basic premise was that an individual's personality goes through structural elaborations in accord with a ground plan which is called the epigenesis (Sprinthall & Sprinthall, 1987). As a person grows, he or she encounters eight stages of psychosocial crises. Each stage is characterized by a unique bi-polar dimension. In this framework or life cycle of psychosocial growth (Sprinthall & Sprinthall, 1987), Erikson named the major conflicting aspects of each period. This helped to disentangle and balance developmental theory as a means of understanding personal growth. To develop a fully functioning and totally coordinated psychosocial identity, one must successfully synthesize the competing alternative at each stage. Issues of success are related to the first five stages of Erikson's developmental model displayed in Table 1 on page 109.

Erikson described the process of "identity formation," or Stage 5, as the focal point for adolescents (Sprinthall & Collins, 1988). At Stage 5, *Identity Moratorium and Achievement versus Continued Diffusion*, the adolescent explores and affirms belief systems and basic values. If life roles and beliefs cannot be resolved, the result can be ego diffusion.

As an adolescent begins to think about self and identity, he or she can:

1. differentiate feelings and emotions in self and others;
2. distinguish between objective and subjective reality;
3. adopt the perspective of another person;
4. understand symbolic meaning and role-play as-if situations (Sprinthall & Sprinthall, 1987, p. 144).

In order to facilitate growth and the resolution of the Stage 5 dichotomy (identity versus identity diffusions), an additional cognitive developmental counseling model which operates from a theoretical frame of positivism should be used.

The African-American female is caught in a "double-bind" because of her race and gender. These traits are not valued in our society. Therefore, it is important to promote a positive sense of self, to attempt to help her resolve negative roles and beliefs, and to adopt a positive perspective.

Evaluating Self-Esteem in the African-American Female

Ladner (cited in Jeffries, 1976) conducted a study of over 100 adolescent African-American females from poor and urban environments in an attempt to redefine the psychosocial phases of African-American female development. Her study revealed that the African-American female is socialized into womanhood at an accelerated pace as compared to her non-African-American peers. Ladner's subjects were concerned with paramount issues of survival. Ladner pointed out that peer groups should be used to serve as a clearinghouse for ideas and as a judge or evaluator for scrutinizing various ideas regarding the best or most appropriate form of behavior in a given situation.

Jeffries (1976) stated that the counselor who works with African-American female adolescents can use the support of peer group relationships to lessen the labor of problem solving. An additional suggestion from Jeffries was for the counseling psychologist to focus on the strengths of the African-American female client and to help her discover a career that raises her level of self-efficacy so she knows she is capable of joining the work force.

Jeffries noted that:

the counseling psychologist can, therefore, assist the black female client to increase her competencies and take advantage of her 'double-negative equals positive' position in the job market (p. 21).

Kirk (1975) proffered the following African-American developmental model of the evolution of high self-esteem as a guide for counselors:

Stage One: Self-depreciating
African-Americans in the first stage spend most of their time criticizing others who may sound better or disagree with their point of view. Their behavior is self-effacing and characterized by hate, prejudice, low self-esteem, hostility, and fear.

Stage Two: Self-pity
African-Americans in this stage are still denying the self and attempting to affirm their ethnicity. Their behavior is self-indulgent. The world seems to be an evil and hostile place.

Stage Three: Self-examination
The third stage provides African-Americans an opportunity to explore their cultural heritage from Africa to America. The knowledge one acquires engenders self-endorsement and empowerment. They learn to interpret the negative and positive feedback from the cultural environment. These African-Americans try out new roles and images, searching for the one to add to their personal repertoire.

Stage Four: Self-knowledge
At this level, one finds ambivalence diminishing and self-confidence rising. African-Americans are working toward a common cause. Conversations regarding politics, racism, and unity are prevalent; they show fewer negative and irrational behaviors. The focus is on strengthening their individual identities.

Stage Five: Self-esteem
The fifth stage finds the African-American has achieved personal and social identity, and has pride in their ethnic heritage. At this stage, the person has learned to play an intricate role in society, and has a sanguine outlook on life. They feel they are valuable, effectual, and necessary citizens and they relate powerfully to the external world.

The psychosocial development frameworks of Kirk (1975) and Erikson (cited in Sprinthall & Collins, 1987; Sprinthall & Sprinthall, 1988) can serve as a guide for the career assessment of African-American female athletes. Jeffries (1976) argued that:

> The assumption that the African-American woman is operating from the weakest social position in society prevents the psychologist from helping her to rally her positive qualities, and thus decreases her ability to resolve her presenting problem (p. 21).

The counselor who utilizes both the cognitive developmental and cognitive behavioral model could capture the essence of the career dilemma exhibited by the African-American female athlete.

Social Cognitive Model

Albert Bandura (1982) formulated his social cognitive theory in which performance of behavior is determined by interdependent interaction between three major factors: situations, behavior and cognition. Self-efficacy, or the belief about one's own ability to successfully perform a given behavior, is the significant underpinning to the social cognitive theory.

Bandura (1982) postulated that efficacy expectations helped to determine whether behavior will be initiated, how much effort will be expended, and how long effort will be sustained when faced with tense situations.

Efficacy expectations are acquired through enactive attainment or self and outcome efficacies; vicarious learning experiences, modeling or observational learning; verbal persuasion, or self and outcome efficacies; and one's physiological state or the interaction between the person and the environment (Bandura, 1982 & 1986). The cognitive factors are fused within a self-regulatory process which decisively impacts human behavior.

Bandura (cited in Lent & Hackett, 1987) visualized self-efficacy as shifting along three dimensions; *level, strength,* and *generality.*

Level refers to the degree of difficulty of the tasks or behaviors that an individual feels capable of performing. *Strength* refers to the confidence a person has in his or her performance estimates. *Generality of self-efficacy* concerns the range of situations in which a person considers him or herself efficacious.

The concept of "collective efficacy" or shared precepts of efficacy within groups of people (Bandura, 1982) can significantly impact African-American female athletes. Cultural groups can internalize covert self-deprecating messages communicated via sociopolitical forces which may, in turn, affect their career behavior. Lent and Hackett (1987) provided the following example:

> To the extent that certain minority students receive inadequate or biased exposure to information necessary for developing strong precepts of career self-efficacy, environment-imposed barriers may become internalized. In turn, weak efficacy beliefs may limit the level of future performance one is willing to attempt and the degree to which one will persevere under stressful conditions. Low precepts of ability are thereby reinforced (p. 373).

Thus, a career intervention, which is within the context of cognitive developmental and the social cognitive domains, can be effective in enhancing the level of self-efficacy and formulating a strong identity for the African-American female athlete. The primary purpose of the intervention would be to help African-American female athletes move to level five on the Erikson and Kirk scales with a fully functioning identity-achieved ego.

Cognitive Developmental and Social Cognitive Intervention

Exum (1986, p. 113) notes that intervention is based on the following assumptions:

> (1) that the stress and general disequilibrium experienced by many Black women at predominantly white institutions are the result of conflicts between

their expectations of the academic environment and their actual experiences in academia. They essentially experience culture shock;

(2) that the disequilibrium itself is not necessarily negative, but the adjustments made to the disequilibrium may be negative; and

(3) that part of the successful resolution of these conflicts can be facilitated through a rational balancing of academic, social/emotional, and physical activities.

The author suggested that the goal of intervention is to increase the woman's level of self-efficacy and personal command of the academic environment.

Real Life Experiences

Strategies that counselors and therapists could implement to help the African-American female athlete become more self-efficacious in her career decision making skills are as follows:

Expose the athletes to successful individuals who were former athletes and/or coaches. This is a variable in Bandura's social learning theory known as modeling or vicarious learning experiences. Abney's (1989) dissertation examined the effects of role models on career patterns of African-American women. She found that for the vast majority of women, their lives were devoid of a career mentor. It was noted that family members made a significant impact in the careers of women. Most of the African-American women interviewed in this study had acted as mentors, were committed to mentoring, and strongly believed that having a mentor is an aid to a young woman at the outset of her career.

A mentor program could be established. Former African-American alumni who played collegiate sports can facilitate workshops on coping strategies in the work world, developing and enhancing students' self-concept, and can also provide assistance on successfully matriculating through the university.

Athletes can be paired with a mentor for an academic year. The mentor could work one-on-one with the athlete and provide additional support via personal counseling, networking, and exposure to the work environment. The athlete would have an opportunity to watch and observe those who have contributed to their alma mater and are making their mark in the "real world" as well.

Reflection

Athletes can be asked to do the following as part of the student mentor and assistance program: The athlete is asked to keep a written journal of important thoughts, feelings and emotions, or incidents that happen to her on a daily basis. She is also asked to reflect upon her goals, dreams, and aspirations as often as possible. Steps to achieve her goals, pitfalls, and the academic credentials needed to attain her objectives can be provided by her counselor. The counselor or therapist should review the journal on a weekly basis, with the primary goal of this exercise being to elicit some emotional arousal from the student athlete. The counselor can desensitize excessive career choice or performance anxiety (Lent & Hackett, 1987) and strengthen the self-concept by commenting in the appropriate areas of the journals. If the athlete meets with her mentor, she should indicate her experiences and point out what stood out for her that day.

Balance and Support

Once per month, athletes should attend a workshop with their counselor and peers. They should process, explore, and discuss career options, and encourage each person to strive for challenging goals. This form of verbal persuasion is presented by Bandura (1977, 1986). Positive self-talk, enlisting the encouragement of others is a form of "collective efficacy." By sharing and inculcating positive messages regarding ability, intellect, and self-concept, the African-American female athlete can share in a dream of career success and make a significant contribution to society.

Challenge

This form of performance accomplishment would involve the athlete in various role-taking situations in a coached atmosphere to ensure completion. Exercises could include a mock job interview with mentor, volunteer or internship activity in the athlete's academic field, mentoring an African-American female athlete who is in middle school or high school, or acquiring and exploring new information on various career fields related to the athletes academic pursuits. Continuous feedback and support should be given by peers, the counselor, and mentors.

Conclusion

The concerns raised and intervention described in this paper is intended to help prepare the African-American female athlete for a successful transition from an athletic and campus environment to a career and help her move from an identity-diffused to an identity-achieved state. The role of the counselor is to support, challenge, empower, encourage, and abet in the psychosocial development of the African-American female college athlete.

Programming must be designed at every school to help the African-American female athlete proceed to an identity-achieved status, in possession of a positive self-concept.

TABLE I

Erickson's Ground Plan for Psychosocial Growth

Age	Bipolar Crisis for Each Stage (Outlined)				
Birth to twenty-four months	Basic trust vs. mistrust	Early autonomy, etc.	Early initiative	Early mastery	Early identity
Two to three years	Later forms of hope, etc.	Autonomy vs. shame			
Four to six years		Later forms of will	Initiative vs. guilt		
Six to twelve years			Later forms of purpose	Mastery vs. inferiority	
Thirteen to Eighteen years				Later forms of competence	Identity vs. diffusion
Eighteen years through college					Identity (Moratorium and achievement) vs. continued diffusion
Resolution	**Hope**	**Will**	**Purpose**	**Competence**	**Fidelity**

Sprinthall, N.A. & Sprinthall, R.C. (1987). *Educational psychology: A developmental approach.* (4th edition). New York: Random House.

References

Abney, R. (1989). *The effects of role models and mentors on career patterns of black women coaches and athletic administrators in historically black and historically white institutions of higher education* (Doctoral dissertation, University of Iowa, 1988). Dissertation Abstracts International, 49, 3210A.

Alexander, J. (1979). *Psychological and emotional stress on the Black male student athlete: An analysis and some strategies for relief.* (Psychological and Vocational Counseling Center Monograph Series No. 3). Gainesville: University of Florida Psychological and Vocational Counseling Center.

Ames, N. (1984). "The socialization of women into and out of sports." *Journal of NAWDAC,* 3-7.

Anthony-Perez, B. (1985). "Institutional racism and sexism: Refusing the legacy in education." In Treichler, P.A., Kramarae, C., & Stafford, B.(Eds.), *For alma mater: theory and practice in feminist scholarship* (pp. 209-217). Urbana, Il: University of Illinois Press.

Balazs, E., & Nickerson, E. (1976)." A personality needs profile of some outstanding female athletes." *Journal of Clinical Psych.,* 32, 45-49.

Bandura, A. (1982). "Self-efficacy: Toward a unifying theory of behavioral change." *Psychological Review,* 84, 191-215.

Bandura, A. (1986). *Social foundations of thought and action: A social cognitive theory.* Englewood Cliffs, NJ: Prentice-Hall.

"Blacks under represented in all athletic jobs, survey shows." (1988, October 10). *The NCAA News,* p. 1, 12-13.

Boslooper, T., & Hayes, M. (1973). *The femininity game.* New York: Stein and Day.

Boutilier, M. A., & SanGiovanni, L. (1983). *The sporting woman.* Champaign, Il: Human kinetics.

Bredemeier, B.J. (1983). "Athletic aggression: A moral concern." In Goldstein, J. (Ed.), *Sports violence.* (pp. 47-81). New York: Springer-Verlag.

Carrington, C. H. (1980). "Depression in black women: A theoretical appraisal." In L. F. Rogers-Rose (Ed.), *The black woman* (pp. 265-271). Beverly Hills, Sage Publications.

Clark, V. L., Horton, F., & Alford, R. L. (1986). "NCAA rule 48: Racism or reform." *Journal of Negro Education,* 55, 162-170.

Coakley, J. J. (1978). *Sport in society.* Saint Louis: The C. V. Mosby Company.

Colker, R., & Widom, C. S. (1980). "Correlates of female athletic participation: Masculinity, femininity, self-esteem, and attitudes toward women." *Sex Roles,* 6, 47-58.

Edwards, H. (1970). *Black students.* New York: The Free Press.

Edwards, H. (1973). *Sociology of sport.* Homewood, Il: The Dorsey Press.

Erickson, E. H. (1966). "The concept of identity in race relations: Notes and queries." *Daedalus.* 95, 145-172.

Evans, G. (1988). "The winning ways of Iowa's C. Vivian Stringer." *Black Issues in Higher Education,* 5, 5.

Exum, H. (1986). "Perspectives on counseling Black women in academia." In C. Taylor (Ed.), *Handbook of minority student services* (pp. 112-143). Madison, WI: NMCC Inc.

Farrell, C. S. (1988). "Black students opting out of college baseball: While major leagues recruit from college ranks." *Black Issues in Higher*

Fleming, J. (1989, February 2). "Analyzing the contemporary experience of blacks in college." *Black Issues in Higher Education*, p. 12-16.

Gerdy, J. R. (1987). "No more dumb jocks." *The College Review*, 143, 2-3, 40.

Green, R. L., Smith, G. S., Gunnings, T. S., & McMillan, J. H. (1974a). "Black athletes: Educational, economic, and political considerations." *Journal of Non-White Concerns in Personnel and Guidance*, 3, 6-27.

Green, R. L., Smith, G. S., Gunnings, T. S., & McMillan, J. H. (1974b). "The status of blacks in the Big Ten Athletic Conference: Issues and concerns." *Journal of Non-White Concerns in Personnel and Guidance*, 3, 28-38.

Green, T. S., Olglesby, C. A., Alexander, A., & Franke, N. (Eds.). (1981). *Black women in sport*. Reston, VA: American Alliance for Health, Physical Education, Recreation and Dance.

Greenberg, R. J. (1984). "AIAW vs. NCAA: The take-over and implications." *Journal of NAWDAC*, 29-36.

Greendorfer, J. L. (1987). "Gender bias in theoretical perspectives: The case of female socialization into sport." *Psychology of Women Quarterly*, 11, 327-340.

Greendorfer, S. (1983)." Shaping the female athlete: The impact of the family." In. M. A. Boutilier, & L. SanGiovanni (Eds.), *The sporting woman* (pp. 135-156). Champaign, Il: Human Kinetics.

Griffin, P. S. (1984). "But she's so feminine: Changing mixed messages we give to girls and women in sports." *Journal of NAWDAC*, 9-12.

Halpert, F. E. (1988, October). "You call this adorable? An open letter to the producer of NBC sports." *Ms.*, pp. 36-39.

Hanks, M. (1979). "Race, sexual status and athletics in the process of educational achievement." *Social Science Quarterly*, 60, 482-496.

Harris, M. M. (1981). *Women's studies and the curriculum*. Salem College.

Higginson, D. C. (1985). "The influence of socialization agents in the female sport-participation process." *Adolescence*, 20, 73-82.

Hoferek, M. J., & Hanick, P. L. (1985). "Women and athlete: Toward role consistency." *Sex Roles*, 12, 687-695.

Horvath, T. (1985). *Basic statistics for behavioral sciences*. Boston: Little, Brown and Company.

Isaac, S., & Michael, W. B. (1985). *Handbook in research and evaluation (2nd ed.)*. San Diego: Edits Publishers.

Jeffries, D. (1976). "Counseling for the strengths of the Black woman." *The Counseling Psychologist*, 6, 20-22.

"Kersees Winning Together. "(1988, September 30). *The News and Observer*. p. 5B.

Kirk, W. (1975). "Where are you? Black mental health model." *Journal of Non-White Concerns in Personnel and Guidance*, 9, 177-188.

Kort, M. (1988, October). "Go, Jackie, go." *Ms.*, pp. 31-33.

Lent, R. W., & Hackett, G. (1987). "Career self-efficacy: Empirical status and future directions." *Journal of Vocational Behavior*, 30, 347-382.

Malone, R. M., & Malone, J. A. (1988). "Two counselors view proposal 48: How a New York college assists athletes." *NASPA Journal*, 25, 249-256.

McDavis, R. J., & Parker, W. M. (1981). "Strategies for helping ethnic minorities with career development." *Journal of Non-White Concerns in Personnel and Guidance, 9*, 130-136.

Mottinger, S. G., & Gench, B. E. (1984). "Comparison of salaries of female and male intercollegiate basketball coaches: An equal opportunity study." *Journal of NAWDAC*, 23-28.

Nation, J. R., & LeUnes, A. (1983). "A personality profile of the black athlete in college football." *Psychology, A Quarterly Journal of Human Behavior, 20*, 1-3.

Olglesby, C. A. (1981). "Myths and realities of black women in sport." In T. S. Green, C. A. Olglesby, A. Alexander, & N. Franke (Eds.), *Black women in sport* (pp. 1-13). Reston, VA: American Alliance for Health, Physical Education, Recreation and Dance.

Petipas, A., & Champagne, D. E. (1988). "Developmental programming for intercollegiate athletics." *Journal of College Student Development, 29*, 454-460.

Potera, C., & Kort, M. (1987). "Are women coaches an endangered species?" *On Campus With Women, 16*, p. 9.

Powell, G. J. (1979). "Growing up Black and female." In C. B. Kopp (Ed.), *Becoming female: Perspectives on development* (pp. 29-66). New York: Plenum.

Rao, P. V. V., & Overman, S. J. (1984)." Sex role perceptions among black female athletes and non-athletes." *Sex Roles, 11*, 601-614.

Sage, G. H., & Loudermilk, S. (1979). "The female athlete and role conflict." *Research Quarterly, 50*, 88-96.

Sapiro, V. (1987). "What research on the political socialization of women can tell us about the political socialization of people." In C.

Farnham (Ed.), *The impact of feminist research in the academy,* (pp. 148-173). Bloomington, IN: Indiana University Press.

Schafer, C. (1989, December 28). "Toys: What are their effects on children?" *Guidepost*, pp. 1, 3, 5.

Selby, H. (1989, June 25). "Playing the gender game." *Raleigh News and Observer*, pp. 1C, 12C.

Simmons, C. (Sr. Producer), & Rhodes, F. T. (Director). (1989). *The Budweiser Sports Report* [Television]. Washington, D.C.: Black Entertainment Television.

Uhlir, G. A. (1984). "For whom the dollars toll." *Journal of NAWDAC*, 1-22.

Urdang, L. & Flexner, S. B. (Eds.). (1968). *The Random House Dictionary of the English language.* New York: Random House.

Walters, S. A., & Stivers, E. (1977). "The relation of student teachers' classroom behavior and Eriksonian ego identity." *Journal of Teacher Education, 28*, 47-50.

Wiggins, D. K. (1985). "From plantation to playing field: Historical writings on the black athlete in American sport." *Research Quarterly for Exercise and Sport, 57*, 101-116.

Williams, A., Jr. (1983). "The impact of rule 48 upon the black student athlete: A comment." *Journal of Negro Education, 52*, 362-373.

Wittig, A. F. (1984). "Sport competition anxiety and sex role." *Sex Roles, 10*, 469-473.

Wittmer, J., Bostic, D., Phillips, R. D., & Waters, W. (1981). "The personal, academic, and career problems of college student athletes: Some possible answers." *The Personnel and Guidance Journal*, 52-55.

Yardley, J. (1988, September 18). "SAT 'bias' isn't the real outrage." The News and Observer, 7D.

Empowering Minority Students for Diversity in the 1900's: A Framework and a Process

ABOUT THE AUTHOR:

Forrest D. Toms

Forrest D. Toms is the Director of the Institute for Multicultural Education and Training, Advisor to the President for Multicultural Affairs, and Assistant Professor of Psychology at Lenoir-Rhyne College, Hickory, North Carolina. He is a doctoral candidate in developmental psychology at Howard University; received his M.A. in psychology and his B.S. in psychology and secondary education from Middle Tennessee State University, Murfreesboro; and his A.A. in general education from Spartanburg Methodist College, Spartanburg, S.C.

Mr. Toms has an extensive background in the areas of multicultural program design, development, and training for non-minorities and ethnic and racial minority groups. Mr. Toms is founder and president of Training Research Development (TRD) Inc., and has lectured and conducted training workshops throughout the country.

ABOUT THE AUTHOR:

Theodore G. White, III

Theodore "Ted" G. White, III is the Assistant Director of the Institute for Multicultural Education and Training (I MET) at Lenoir-Rhyne College, Hickory, North Carolina. He received his Bachelor of Science Degree in History/Political Science from Austin Peay State University, Clarksville, Tennessee and the Master of Arts Degree in Student Personnel Services from Memphis State University, Memphis, Tennessee.

Throughout his professional career, he has served in various capacities that focused on Afro-American student recruitment, retention, development, and community service. Some of these experiences include: 1) Director of Student Organizations and Minority Affairs at Middle Tennessee State University: 2) Coordinator of Athletic/Academic Support Program at Memphis State University; and, 3) Admissions Counselor (First Ethnic/Racial Minority College Recruiter) at Austin Peay State University.

Mr. White has played a central role in the development and successful implementation of the following programs:1)Afro-American Student Development and Enrichment Program; 2) Multicultural Adjustment and Development Program (MCAP); 3) Leadership and Development Training Institute for Afro-American Youth; and, 4) Multicultural Education and Enrichment Training Institute (MEET).

INTRODUCTION

A number of forces and trends face America's educational system. None are as pervasive and encompassing as the issue of diversity and change. The term diversity implies change; in the universities and elsewhere, the change which must occur is proactive and pervasive: new policies which recognize and respect the tremendous ethnic and social diversity both on-and off-campus.

Minority students on white campuses are expected to participate in the mainstream of activity at the same time that they are encountering barriers and attitudes which stand in their way of doing so. This conflict exacerbates the attrition rate for minority students. In addition, few minority students attempt to avail themselves of the opportunity to involve themselves in various campus organizations.

In response, the authors offer a top-to-bottom empowerment process for minority student leaders and student organizations.

This article addresses issues of diversity and change relative to minority student leaders and minority student organizations. It provides insight for educational personnel on issues of diversity and change, ethnic identity development, and, most significantly, strategic planning and development with minority student leaders and organizations.

Also discussed is the need to empower minority student leaders and minority student organizations to adapt, adjust, and move proactively in the reality of diversity in the 1990s and beyond.

EMPOWERING MINORITY STUDENTS FOR DIVERSITY IN THE 1990s:

A Framework and a Process

by
Forrest D. Toms
and Theodore G. White III

Meeting the needs of an increasingly multicultural populace is a difficult challenge for educational institutions. The task will change minority group members; non-minority administrators, faculty and students; and the structure and function of educational institutions.

Diversity is not limited to the United States. Ethnic revitalization movements have evolved around the world. Poland, China, Germany, and the USSR have all experienced various ethnic revitalization movements in the past decade. The issues in all revitalization movements are acceptance of diversity, freedom, pluralism, and change.

Most educators agree diversity is a goal of all educational institutions. However, agreeing with the concept of diversity is quite different from participating in the process of achieving diversity.

Diversity means different things to different people. More than anything else, the term diversity implies change; a top-to-bottom, multifaceted change. In the 1990s this change must involve different tasks for different groups. For minority group members, change means maintaining their ethnic identity while increasing skills necessary for participation in mainstream American society. For White Americans, change means addressing issues of prejudice and racism. For educational institutions, the task of change requires developing a process in which change may occur. Institutions must proactively set forth policies and procedures that reflect their diverse populations. Institutions must develop strategies to combat racism and prejudice on campus (Toms, 1988).

Creating a climate conducive to the development of multicultural perspectives and relationships involves allowing a dynamic process of change. This change process is not mechanical. It is a fluid and continuous process that pervades the core of the institution. The process empowers individuals and institutions as they become more aware, knowledgeable, and effective in addressing issues of diversity. No issue confronting America's educational system is as pervasive and encompassing as the issue of diversity and change.

Minority Student Adjustment

Research indicates that minority students are expected to participate in the mainstream of the institution in the same ways as do non-minority students. Yet, they are confronted with issues and concerns that are drastically different from their white counterparts (Pounce, 1988; Fleming, 1984). Christoffel (1986) contends the additional obstacles encountered by minority students who attend predominantly white colleges exacerbate minority student attrition. For African-Americans and other ethnic and racial minority students, these obstacles are not simply institutional or personal in nature; they are also ethnic and cultural (Toms, 1986).

Numerous factors affect minority student adjustment and development. These factors are both external (e.g., institutional racism, cultural racism, insensitivity to minority student needs, monoculturalism, a workforce which is ill-prepared in dealing with diversity) and internal (e.g., identity development, bi-culturality, adaptive coping strategies).

Recent research relative to the problems minority students encounter at predominantly White institutions indicates that some of the problems are indeed unique to minority students (Pounce, 1988; Fleming, 1984). The most frequently reported concerns include: adjustment to college; academic performance; financial resources; feelings of isolation and loneliness; racial ethnic identity development; racial hostility in the form of harassment; feelings of entitlement (related to a feeling of not deserving to be in college); and the lack of a connection to the college environment (Fleming, 1984; Valdez, Baron, Pounce, 1987; Sedlacek and Brooks, 1976).

Studies conducted of American-Indian, Asian-American, African-American, and Hispanic students at predominantly White educational institutions clearly identify both social and psychological factors that affect the adjustment, development, and retention of minority students. A central theme voiced by minority students from each group is that of social and cultural isolation (Lunneborg and Lunneborg, 1986). In fact, some researchers suggest that predominantly White educational institutions isolate more than they educate(West and de la Teja, 1988; Fleming, 1984).

Students attending higher educational institutions, regardless of race or ethnicity, experience loneliness and worry about their academic performance and social involvement while adjusting to college. However, as Fleming (1984) points out,

> If college students, in general, face developmental and social adaptation challenges, what outcomes can be expected for those who come to college with a special set of characteristics that they must reconcile within existing educational environments?

In her book, *Blacks in College*, Fleming (1984) concluded the following regarding Blacks matriculating on predominantly Black versus predominantly White universities:

1. Development among White students in White colleges roughly parallels that of Black students in Black colleges.

2. Black male development suffers the most at predominantly White campuses. On predominantly Black campuses, Black men occupy turf that is comparable to that of White men on White campuses.

3. Black women are more assertive on predominantly White campuses, while less likely to be assertive on predominantly Black campuses.

4. Predominantly Black colleges positively influenced Black students' cognitive develop-

ment, intellectual development, and inter-personal development.

5. Predominantly White colleges have not succeeded in combatting Black students' social isolation, perception of classroom biases, and perceptions of hostile interpersonal climates.

These findings and others clearly indicate that minority students fare better socially, culturally, and intellectually at predominantly Black institutions.

Harper (1969) suggests there is a trauma to being Black and feeling alone on a predominantly White college campus. Taylor (1986) suggested an urgency of building a Black identity in environments where Blacks are present, whether in the form of African-American studies or other programs. Blacks and other racial minority group members who aspire for equality and opportunity in traditional education areas can expect adjustment difficulties. Lastly, the changing demographics and the projected increase in minority students will require educators and institutions to develop support networks for minority students which are culturally relative. These systems must be comprehensive in design and implementation. They must educate and sensitize non-minority administrators, faculty, and students, while empowering minority students with a sense of their cultural heritage and the skills necessary for participation in the mainstream (Toms, 1988).

More recently, Boykin (1983, 1985) offered a framework for understanding the African-American experience. All members of ethnic minority groups experience some form of racism and discrimination as they participate in the mainstream of American life but he contends that African-Americans face a triple quandary.

First, African-Americans are likely to be incompletely socialized to the Euro-American cultural ethos;

Secondly, they typically develop stylistic repertoires which arise out of their African heritage; and

Thirdly, they are victimized by racial and economic oppression.

The triple quandary that African-Americans experience, Boykin suggests, is the product of interplay between the mainstream experience, the minority experience, and the African-American cultural experience. The triple quandary exists for any African-American; however, not all cope with these experiences in the same way (Toms and Boykin, 1986). Ethnic groups and individuals react, adjust, and develop adaptive reactions and coping strategies in their own particular ways.

In effect, there is a certain inescapable duality that exists in being African-American and participating in mainstream America. Jones (1986) speaks of this duality in terms of a bifurcation of self process. He suggests that it presents psychic conflict when it produces an approach-avoidance tension at a single instant; or, it may be a source of situational adaptation when one selectively calls upon the self that is most suited to handle a given situation. James Baldwin (1963) captures this notion of a dual orientation as:

> That of experiencing one's self through the eyes of another group of people who are culturally, socially, and psychologically different.

Nevertheless, African-Americans and other minorities show evidence of embracing mainstream American ethos and participating in and being influenced by mainstream American institutions (Boykin and Toms, 1985). Frederikson (1982) maintains that entering the mainstream implies more than economic entry; it also suggests the adoption of the ideologies of the mainstream society. Frederikson further asserts that:

> Conditionality of mainstream entry which is based on willingness to identify with the aims and ideologies of

the White dominated institution...which may create a dilemma of identity for Black intellectuals and high achievers (p.24).

The opinions on why African-American and other ethnic minority groups are experiencing adjustments difficulties at higher levels than their non-minority counterparts are as diverse as the adjustment problems themselves. Regardless, the fact is that the numbers of African-Americans in colleges and universities are dwindling.

Minority Student Organizations

It is believed by many educators and social scientists that student involvement (Astin, 1984) and integration into the fabric of the college experience (Tinto, 1975) contributes to student retention. For minority students, however, involvement in campus-wide activities and student organizations has been sparse at best (Garza and Nelson, 1973; Hunt, 1975; Rooney, 1985).

A recent study of Asian-American, African-American, Hispanic, and American Indian students at the University of Wisconsin-Madison shows that while 70% were aware of minority student organizations and 62% indicated a positive attitude toward such groups, only 17% reported actually being involved (Rooney, 1985). The study indicated that the two most important reasons for minority student involvement were interaction with others from the same background and the opportunity to make friends. The most important reason given by Asian-Americans, African-Americans, and Hispanics was a need for moral support and help in solving problems. Most significant, perhaps, was the finding that 63% of those minority students not involved in a minority student organization had attended integrated high schools.

As suggested by Chavis (1982), respondents in Rooney's study seem to feel that minority student organizations set them apart from others. This lack of involvement of minority students in minority

student organizations or campus-wide activities and organizations has been attributed to differing interests and goals, perceptions of a lack of receptivity to their participation on the part of the institution and organizations, and the general climate of the campus (Lyons, 1973; Hunt, 1975).

For at least the past two decades, many predominantly White campuses have experienced the emergence of different minority student organizations. These organizations range from African-American, Asian-American, Hispanic, and American Indian student organizations; to fraternities, sororities, alumni societies and associations; and more recently, multicultural centers. These groups and organizations exist at almost every college or university with a sizeable minority student enrollment (Rooney, 1985).

The mission and goals of the organizations vary from campus to campus. However, most serve as social and cultural agents by assisting students in maintaining their cultural identities. They provide culturally relevant extracurricular activities (e.g., workshops, dances, Greek celebrations, and special cultural and ethnic heritage celebrations).

As noted earlier, minority student participation in organizations is extremely low (Rooney, 1985). Many campuses are isolating and alienating to minority students, with workforces and student bodies that are ill-prepared to understand and respect diversity. Therefore, minority student organizations are seen as hospices for minority students on predominantly White college campuses. Moses Turner, Vice President for Student Affairs at Michigan State University, captures the relations between African-American minority student organizations and the educational administration. He states:

So often what happens is, the black fraternities say to the administrators,
"You don't understand us, so why don't you just leave us alone?"
And the university administrators say,

"You know, you're right. We don't understand you, so we will leave you alone" (Rolleson, 1987).

Cindy Price, Assistant Director of Small Group Houses and Greek Life at Bowling Green State University, says that minority student fraternities and sororities "foster leadership and can promote academic excellence." Ronal S. Beer, Vice President for Student Services, characterizes minority student organizations as "the primary social vehicles for blacks." Chavis (1982) suggests that minority student organizations have settled their struggle with identity and are more driven towards participation in campus-wide activities and organizations. Other researchers wonder whether minority student organizations have mastered the mainstream system or if they want to be involved in campus-wide activities. A recent poll (Barol, Camper, Pigott, Nadolsky, and Sarris, 1983) pointed out that minority students prefer their own groups and are not active in campus-wide student organizations.

There are a number of variables that factor into minority students' participation in their own organizations as well as in broader campus activities and organizations. These factors are both internal and external to minority students. They involve issues of identity, alienation, and isolation. They also include perception of the campus climate regarding diversity, perceived racism and lack of receptivity to minority participation, and various adaptive reactions and coping strategies to racism, discrimination, and prejudice.

We contend that variables such as mono-cultural campus environments have an impact on participation. Lack of sensitivity and awareness of the needs of culturally diverse student populations, lack of support systems for minority students, and failure to provide minority students with institutional support keeps minority students from participating fully. A lack of understanding of the variations of the college adjustment process

minority students experience contributes to low involvement and participation in student organizations.

We offer a top-to-bottom empowerment process for minority student leaders and minority organizations. This empowerment process assumes that given the bicultural nature of minority students' existence on campus, feelings of alienation and isolation, and the obstacles to successful adjustment they face, minority students must work proactively to fortify their status on campus. The process starts with the cultural self-awareness of minority student leaders and their respective organizations. It involves increasing their knowledge of their own culture. It also entails developing leadership skills and increasing minority student organizations' participation on key committees and organizations within the broader campus life.

If Astin's (1984, p. 304) contention that changes in attitude and behavior that usually accompany college attendance can be attributed to the peer group effect is correct, then it is imperative that we explore more culturally relative methods of organizing, developing, and training minority group students for leadership roles. The diversity within minority populations in the country and on campuses demands that we take a more systematic and process-oriented approach to student development with minority student leaders and organizations.

Preparing Minority Students for Full Participation in the Academy

Successful participation in the mainstream of educational institutions and society in general involves a preparatory process. This process aids minority students in dealing with their cultural heritage while assisting them in acquiring the necessary knowledge and skills for successful participation within the mainstream of the institution.

Many minority students in predominantly White institutions feel alienated, isolated, and that they are not a part of the mainstream of campus. As a result, minority students tend not to participate in campus-wide events and organizations. The tacit assumption has been that students should come in prepared with the "cultural capital" (Delpit, 1987) to fully participate within the day-to-day functioning of the institution, particularly as it relates to involvement in campus-wide activities and student organizations. If minority students fail to participate, the inferred reasons for this lack of involvement centers around issues of social and cultural deficiencies and differences.

In the past, higher educational institutions and student services personnel in particular have failed to recognize, understand, and value the process of helping minority students make the transition to campus life successfully. This suggests that institutions have not put a well-conceived process in place to include students in the planning and development of all types of social and cultural activities on the campus calendar. This lack of participation is presupposed by many variables such as the institution's inability to develop and maintain culturally relevant services for minority students and a general insensitivity to minority student needs.

This process of preparing minority students for full participation at educational institutions must be conceptualized and implemented on two separate levels simultaneously. First, it means the institution's leadership must understand that empowering minority student leaders and minority student organizations will have a positive effect on the overall recruitment, development, and retention of minority students. That is, when minority student leaders are empowered to understand and feel comfortable with themselves and with majority peers, then they will take on additional leadership responsibilities within the institution. These same individuals will be more willing to assist in recruitment. Also, the institutional leadership must

develop a comprehensive cultural awareness program to prepare its workforce to deal with the realities of cultural diversity in the next decade.

On a second level, the preparation process must also involve providing minority student leaders with information on the institution's overall functioning. For instance, what offices provide services to minority students? What offices maintain funding for minority students to bring in guest speakers? What offices set the major policies on student life activities? What offices are charged with recruiting and retaining minority students on the predominantly White campus? This is the kind of information that minority students will need to know about the top to bottom structural functioning of the institution, particularly as it relates to the politics of the institution and their being able to fit into the day-to-day reality of that institution.

This process involves team-building and group-building with African-American and other minority student leaders. The process begins with training sessions that address issues of identity development, cultural racial awareness, ethnic or racial group heritage, planning and development. Also, as a part of the training process, these student leaders will develop a one-year, three-year, and five-year plan. The sessions will teach student leaders how to organize their peers around certain issues and assist them in systematically developing strategies to achieve their goals despite roadblocks that may inhibit the growth and development of minority students and their organizations.

The Empowerment Process

Empowerment is a process by which people become better able to influence those persons and organizations that affect their lives and the lives of those they care about (London, 1990). The process of becoming empowered provides individuals and organizations with the psychological, social, and cognitive resources to remove structural and functional barriers which may impede their efforts to achieve and progress.

Empowerment as a concept and process must be understood from a multi-faceted perspective, particularly when we speak of the educational empowerment of minority student leaders and organizations.

The process of empowerment involves change not only for the disempowered group, but also the dominating group. Educational empowerment, according to London (1990), appears to be a logical requirement for all who are involved in the process of educating a child. Cummins (1986) provides a framework for empowering minority students. He suggests that educators redefine the way they interact with minority children and the communities they serve. The implementation of change is dependent upon the extent to which educators, both collectively and individually, redefine their roles with respect to minority students and communities. Further, he submits that even though legislative and political reform may be necessary conditions for effective change, they are not sufficient in themselves.

When we speak of empowering minority student leaders and student organizations, the responsibility for change must not only include minority students. It must include leadership from the administrators, support from the faculty, staff, and the general student body. The educational leadership is responsible for change, which involves changing the attitudes of faculty and students regarding minority students. It involves planning new positive relationships between minority students, minority communities, and the institution. It involves promoting other programs and incentives that reflect diversity and pluralism.

The goals of the empowerment process are to:

1. Assist minority student organizations in further development of effective organizational structures, planning processes, and program development strategies;

2. Assist minority student organizations in providing cultural enrichment programs for colleges and communities;

3. Promote a feeling of belonging and accountability among minority student organization members to the mission of developing, enrolling, and retaining minority students on predominantly white campuses;

4. Increase the participation and visibility of minority students in their organizations and in broader campus life;

5. Assist minority student organizations and individuals with developing skills needed to successfully participate in the mainstream of the institution while providing them with support to maintain and strengthen their heritage, cultural and ethnic identity.

6. Educate minority student organizations to the services and resources available to them at predominantly white colleges.

Phases of the Empowerment Process

Phase I: Selecting Participants: The Foundation

The first phase of the minority student empowerment process involves identifying, contacting, and organizing minority student organizational leaders. On campuses where there are significant numbers of different ethnic and racial cultural minority groups, only the officers of each are part of the initial planning and development. Generally, the President, Vice President, Secretary, Treasurer, and, in some cases, committee chairpersons, are involved at this point. It will also be helpful to include students who have emerged as leaders, via the informal network, but who may not actually be a leader in one of the organizations on campus (e.g., athlete, musician--students who are very popular and exhibit a sense of group consciousness).

This particular phase is critical. Several objectives must be achieved in the first two meetings of the group. First, the facilitator must create an atmosphere of openness, excitement, and interest to students. Make sure the goals of the groups are clear, concise, and believed to be achievable. Provide students with exercises for getting acquainted and team-building. Assist students in identifying problems and concerns of minority students on campus generally, and specifically as they relate to increasing participation of minority students in minority student organizations.

A major focus of Phase I is to help students understand the need for minority student organizations to fortify themselves as a group through collective efforts, become more of a support system for their student peers, understand the process of developing partnerships and working relationships with different organizations, and understand the relationship between a collective effort of minority student leaders and organizations to providing more recognition and participation of minority students in the mainstream of campus life.

The achievement of the objectives in the first phase involves a great deal of networking with student leaders before and after the first few meetings. It also means disseminating information through letters, telephone calls, and taking meals with students in the cafeteria. Gatherings at the home of minority faculty and staff may be favorable.

Phase II: Level I

Phase II is process-oriented. It involves two areas of focus: 1) Awareness-and knowledge-building; and 2) Leadership development training. The major objective of Phase II is to increase the overall awareness, knowledge, and skills of minority group leaders, as well as their organizational competence to meet the needs of their peers.

The awareness- and knowledge-building level centers around a structured plan to increase student cultural self-awareness, knowledge of their cultural or racial heritage, and knowledge of mainstream structures. The plan also aims to increase students' adaptive coping strategies to racism, bias, prejudices, and indifference.

The first part of awareness training focuses on identity development and cultural heritage. Workshops and training sessions are held biweekly to discuss topics such as: *The psychology of the African-American experience; Biculturality, or Living in two different worlds at the same time;* and *Exercises in critical analysis and thinking.* Thus, Level I of Phase II is based on developing a year-long academic calendar that has structured meetings where minority students can increase their knowledge of their cultural heritage. These meetings include lectures, discussions, films and videos, small group exercises, field trips, and selected presentations on campus and in the community.

Phase II: Level II

This level involves preparing students to be more effective and representative leaders within their particular organizations and of minority students in general. This level is composed of knowledge-building, leadership-development activities, and experiential planning and development exercises.

In the knowledge-building component, the focus is on knowing and understanding the structure and function of key organizations and offices (both student-related and administrative) that are responsible for student activities and services, and provide financial assistance to all student organizations. This includes student government officers, committees, the Vice President for Academic Affairs, the President, the Student Affairs' office, special events committees, and housing. Knowing how to get things done at an institution is critical for minority students. It will ensure that their interest becomes even more important in Phase III.

Phase II also includes a focus on leadership development skills. The major objective centers on assisting students in identifying and developing effective leadership styles and methods. Attention is drawn to the information acquired in the experiences of Phase I. This reflects the tremendous amount of diversity that exists among minority students in their level of cultural awareness and differences in coping strategies related to being a minority on a predominately white campus. By understanding the nature of the diversity of their peers, student leaders can better respond to the needs of minority students. They can also better understand what issues face student organizations.

The third area of Phase II addresses planning and development. Planning and development requires conducting a needs assessment of the student leaders. This needs assessment asks student leaders to identify:

1) Five major problem areas or concerns of minority students on campus;

2) Major strengths and weaknesses of minority student leaders;

3) Major strengths and weaknesses of minority student organizations;

4) Goals of minority student organizations (one-year, three-year and five-year goals) both the goals of each particular organization and the group goals for all minority students;

5) A list of strategies to achieve each of the goals listed; and to develop

6) An academic year calendar for minority students with month-to-month timelines.

After the process of fortification and empowerment in Phase II, minority student leaders are now ready for full participation in campus-wide leadership and activities. That is, the process of increasing minority students' awareness, knowledge, and leadership skills prepares them for full representative leadership of all minority students.

At this point, these minority student leaders have acquired a sense of ethnic group consciousness and integrity as well as a working knowledge of campus politics. They have gained an understanding that adaptive coping strategies are necessary to deal with indifference and a lack of concern for minority student needs. They move proactively to cope with racism, bias, and prejudice. They have a clear understanding of their role and objectives in representing minority student needs. They have the assessment, planning, and development skills needed to be effective leaders.

Through this process of empowerment, minority student leaders will be equipped with the knowledge, confidence, and skills necessary to be effective agents for change as they become more visible and active participants in the mainstream of institutional life.

Phase III: Selection and Placement of Minority Students in Campus-Wide Committees and Offices

The major objective of this phase is to devise strategies to place minority students in various campus-wide committees, offices, and organizations. The idea is to get as much minority student representation as possible in student government offices, special events' committees, concert committees, campus newspaper staff, and any organizations or committees that set policies, determine social activities for the campus, and distribute money to student organizations.

Placing minority students in leadership roles on various committees and in certain organizations ensures that the minority student perspective will play a part in the decision-making process. This representation is critical to the development of successful minority students on campus, and even more so to their White counterparts who will begin to entertain new possibilities about what representative leadership for all students really means. Minority student representation begins the process of achieving and maintaining diversity at all levels within the institution.

Phase IV: Increased Participation in Campus-Wide Activities

This phase is the actualization of the goals and objectives of the first three phases. In this phase, minority students are empowered with a sense of identity and provided with information on the dynamics of the mainstream. They are provided with leadership training with special emphasis on short-term and long-range planning and developmental skills. With this type of training and support, minority students' input can be expected and valued in the context of the overall campus. Prior to making assumptions about why minority students do not participate in campus-wide activities, certain questions must be asked:

Is the campus prepared to accept and work with minority student leaders who may have different needs and visions about the social, cultural, and educational activities on campus?

Have minority students been prepared to take on the responsibility of participating as leaders in the broader campus community? Are support systems in place to assist minority students in developing their leadership skills?

Is there adequate support from advisors of committees and officers of the broader campus community to ensure equal representation in the selection of speakers, performers, and movies for social activities on campus?

Phase V: Impact on Institutions: Increased Awareness and Respect for Diversity

By empowering minority student leaders and organizations, the institution strengthens its ability to recruit, develop, and retain minority students. Secondly, institutions move forward in understanding and respecting minority students and the richness and diversity they bring to campus life. White students, faculty, and administrators increase their awareness and cross-cultural communication skills, and gain interactive skills through increased contact with minority students in environments other than the campus and workplace. In effect, the entire campus environment has more potential for change and growth, thus becoming a more supportive climate both academically and socially for minority student participation and graduation.

Phase VI: Long-Term Implications

The long-term implications of this framework become clearer as institutions proceed through each phase. As a result of the empowerment process, minority student retention is increased. Minority students become more visible through their participation in campus-wide activities. The overall awareness, knowledge, and skills of White faculty, staff, and students are enhanced. The campus climate itself reflects the diversity of all students at the institution.

Other long-term implications include preparing students, both minority and white, with leadership training and the experience of cross-cultural interactions needed to function effectively in the workforce and as community leaders and parents. Students with the experiences and skills of working with culturally diverse groups can be a tremendous resource to any community. The process will provide the foundation for future leadership in both minority and white communities that will be culturally aware, knowledgeable, and experienced in working with diverse people. With a little insight and foresight and a lot of mentoring and education, these students will be the torch bearers of tomorrow, a tomorrow in which diversity is understood and respected.

References

Armstrong-West, S., and de la Teja, M.H. (1988). "Social and Psychological Factors Affecting the Retention of Minority Students." In *From Survival to Success Promoting Minority Student Retention.* M.C. Terrell and D.T. Wright (Eds.), Monograph Series, Volume 9.

Astin, A.W. (1982). *Minorities in American Higher Education.* San Francisco, CA: Jossey-Bass Publishers, Inc.

Astin, A.W. (1984). "Student Development: A Development Theory for Higher Education." *Journal of College Student Personnel,* v.25, pp. 297-308.

Baldwin, J. (1963). "A Talk to Teachers." *Saturday Review,* December 21, pp. 42-44.

Barol, B., Camper, D., Pigott, C. Nadolsky, R., and Sarris, M. (1983). "Separate Tables: Why White and Black Students Choose to Segregate." *Newsweek on Campus*, pp.4-11.

Boykin, A.W. (1983). "The Academic Performances of Afro-American Children." In J.T. Spence (Ed.), *Achievement and Achievement Motives.* San Francisco, CA: W.H. Freeman.

Boykin, A.W. (1985). "The Triple Quandary of Schooling Afro-American Children." In V. Neisser (ed). *The School Achievement of Minority Children.* Hillsdale, NJ: Erlbaum.

Boykin, A.W. and Toms, F.D. (1985). "Black Child Socialization: A Conceptual Framework." In Harriet and John McAdoo (Eds.), *Black Children,* Sage Publications.

Chavis, E. (1982). "Minority Students Involvement in Student Activities." *Association of College Unions International Bulletin,* pp.15-16.

Christoffel, P. (1986). "Minority Student Access and Retention: A Review." *Research and Development Update.* New York: The College Board.

Colleson, MNK. (1987)." Black Fraternities on White Campuses, Accused of Separation, Say They Are Just Misunderstood." *Chronicle of Higher Education,* April.

Cummins, J. (1986)."Empowering Minority Students: A Framework for Intervention." *Harvard Education Review.* Vol. 56, No. 1.

Delpit, L.D. (1988)."The Silenced Dialogue: Power and Pedagogy in Educating Other People's Children." *Harvard Education Review.* Vol. 58, No. 3.

Fleming, J. (1984). *Blacks in College: A Comparative Study of Students' Success in Black and White Institutions.* San Francisco, CA: Jossey-Bass Publishers, Inc.

Frederikson, G. (1982). *The Black Image in the White Mind:* New Directions, pp.20-23.

Harper, F.D. (1969) "Black Student Revolt on the White Campus." *Journal of College Student Personnel,* 10, pp. 291-295.

Hunt, C.L. (1975). "Alternative Patterns of Minority Group Adjustment in the University." *Education Forum*, 39 (2), pp. 137-147.

London, C.B.C. (1990). *Black Issues in Higher Education.* Vol. 16, No. 21, January.

Lunneborg, C. and Lunneborg, P. (1986). "Beyond Prediction: The Challenge of Minority Achievement in Higher Education." *Journal of Multicultural Counseling and Development.* 14, (2) pp. 77-84.

Sedlacek, W.E. and Brooks, G.C., Jr. (1976). *Racism in American Education: A Model of Change.* Chicago, IL: Nelson Hall.

Taylor, C.A. (1986)." Black Students on Predominantly White College Campuses in 1980s." *Journal of College Student Personnel,* 27 (3), pp. 196-201.

Toms, F.D. and Boykin, A.W. (1986). *Psychological Orientations and Adjustments.* Unpublished Manuscript.

Toms, F.D. (1988). *Cultural Racial Awareness Training Experience (CRATE).* Institute for Multicultural Education and Training, Hickory, NC: Lenoir-Rhyne College.

Tinto, V. (1975). "Dropout From Higher Education: A Theoretical Synthesis of Recent Research." *Review of Education Research,* 45, pp. 89-125.

Valdez, L., Baron, A., Jr., Ponce, F.Q. (1987). "Counseling Hispanic Males." In M. Scher, M. Stevens, G. Good, and G. Eichenield (Eds.), *Handbook of Counseling and Psychotherapy with Men.* Beverly Hills, CA: Sage Publications.

Using Alternative Media
to Stimulate Discussion of Race and Ethnic Relations

ABOUT THE AUTHOR:

Linda
Gibson

Ms. Gibson has combined careers in arts, arts administration, and educational media administration. She is currently a program analyst in the Electronic Media and Film program of the New York State Council on the Arts. Ms. Gibson recently served five years as the Director of Media Production, Acquisition, and Distribution at Middlesex County College in New Jersey; immediately prior, she was Assistant Director of Media at Union County College in New Jersey, where she is still an adjunct faculty member in the Communications Department.

Ms. Gibson received her B.A. in Philosophy from Swarthmore College, and worked toward her Master of Communication at the Annenberg School of Communication, the University of Pennsylvania. She has presented papers at a number of conferences, including the 2nd National Conference on Race and Ethnic Relations in American Higher Education. She is past president of the Board of Directors of Women Make Movies, and is currently on the Board of Trustees of the Thomas A. Edison Arts Consortium, which sponsors the Black Maria Film and Video Festival.

Ms. Gibson is also an experimental video artist whose current work explores the relationship between the individual and society. Her work is known for integrating dance and video and has been exhibited at MoMA, the Centre George Pompidou, the AFI Video Festival, and the Athens Video Festival. She has been the recipient of several awards, grants, fellowships, and residencies.

INTRODUCTION

Many administrators find themselves involved in planning and conducting workshops designed to increase understanding between minority and majority students. They often find it difficult to get students to reveal their true feelings and preconceptions, and sometimes find themselves facing groups of students who merely mouth accepted "liberal" phrases. It is important to expose and examine preconceptions and prejudices in a way that does not threaten students, so that true understanding can be served and racial tensions reduced.

Use of alternative media can aid non-threatening discussions of personal and ethnic stereotypes. Because the material is unfamiliar in content and form, discussion can center around the art and the artist instead of the individual taking part in the discussion. For example, intensely personal or autobiographical art can be used to sensitize audience members to issues surrounding race and prejudice, allowing them to be "brought into" the experience of the artist at the same time that they themselves are neither threatened nor revealed.

This article defines "alternative media," describes how one must tailor the art used to the audience and purpose of discussion, and gives an example of how the author has guided such a discussion.

USING ALTERNATIVE MEDIA

to Stimulate Discussion of Race and Ethnic Relations

by
Linda
Gibson

In this essay, I will argue for the use of alternative media to stimulate discussion about issues of race and ethnic relations in institutions of higher education. I will argue that the very reasons why many faculty and administrators may be wary of alternative media -- its obvious differences from what we have learned to expect from television and commercial film -- are the same reasons why it is an invaluable tool in generating discussion. The setting (classroom, dorm, counseling, etc.) will be of less importance than the process of developing the discussion. Therefore, the ideas I will discuss are equally applicable to audiences of students, staff, faculty, or the general public. My discussion of the use of alternative film and video is rooted in the three ways that I encounter it in my professional life. That is, as a producer of alternative media, as a faculty member who uses it in the classroom, and as a former media director of a county college whose responsibilities included software acquisitions. The interplay of these points of view should become clear as the essay continues.

What is Alternative Media?

This is a common question, since so little alternative media is seen in commercial movie theaters, on television, or on cable. Works can be seen occasionally on PBS, on some of the cable networks, or in the art theaters, often at odd hours and with little promotion. On the whole, however, alternative media has remained invisible to the general public.

Alternative media is a form of independent media. There are many definitions of independent media, which often focus on distinguishing it from network television and Hollywood film. Among the characteristics frequently mentioned are grant or personal funding, subjective points of view, and editorial control by the producer. The common denominator is the independence that the creator of independent media has to make arguments, statements, and observations. Bill Moyers is an independent, as is Ayoka Chinzira. What differentiates the work of Ayoka Chinzira, who represents the type of work addressed in this essay, from the work of Bill Moyers? Aside from the size of the budget, an important difference is who the work is made for--a mass audience, or a specific viewer or community.

Another difference is in the degree to which they use the medium to challenge mainstream norms, both in content and in form.

To differentiate the types of independent media, the body of work focused on here will be described as alternative media. It is that part of the body of independent media that carries these distinctions the farthest. Working outside of the producer/client relationship, grant or personal funding allows the producers of alternative media to retain editorial control of the material. It also allows artist-producers the freedom to craft works around a part of a subject without the need to cover all aspects of the subject. The artist-producer can create new "languages" of media to express ideas not easily expressed in the more common media "languages" (in other words -- inventing other forms than the structures/forms of production of television and Hollywood film).

Most of us are used to the language of television, where the message is usually carried in the audio, and the visuals are illustration (how often have you turned on your TV in one room and were able to follow the program while working in another?). In alternative media, the message is often carried by both the visuals and the audio, each carrying complementary, but not identical, information. The message, therefore, becomes the sum of the two. These new languages are a means to challenge audiences into new ways of seeing, thinking, and reacting.

Most importantly, the autonomy of alternative media allows the artist-producer to create statements with a specific, and often personal, point of view. This is not objective media -- this is media that argues that the camera is never objective and that mediamakers should be public with their opinions. This is media as art -- assuming the tradition of the artist speaking directly to a viewer about an "object" of concern.

Alternative media has found its niche in museums, galleries, libraries, universities, and community centers: places of exhibition where the relationship to the viewer complements one of alternative media's primary characteristics. Alternative media often tries to speak directly to the individual viewer. Therefore these exhibition spaces provide an environment where audiences, meeting face to face, can engage in discussion following the work.

Using Alternative Media to stimulate discussion of race and ethnic relations

Alternative media is a type of production used by artists and producers from all racial and ethnic groups to make statements about their experience and/or view of the world. However, for art-makers of color, alternative media has been the forum most open to both them and their point of view. Thus, it is in alternative media that one finds a rich body of work that discusses the experience of being "the other," not through statistics, but as a personal reality that is experienced daily. Today, this body of work includes media by African-Americans, Asians, Latinos, Native Americans, Pacific Islanders, Palestinians and others from the Middle East. Both male and female experiences and points of view can be found. Much of this work focuses on issues of identity, both individual and communal, and explores cultural values, beliefs, and traditions. In some, cultural characteristics that have been viewed as negative by the society at large, and the community itself, are reviewed and redefined. In others, the point of view is both intellectual and emotional. An important component of the aesthetic foundation of much of the work is the incorporation of the traditional aesthetic values of the community into the media language.

Alternative media is also often made with the intention of entering into a dialogue with the viewer. A common theme is the acknowledgement that language shapes our thought, and thereby our action. While some of this work "tells" the viewer of experiences, most of it "shares" this information with the viewer. All of it invites the viewer to react --to agree or to disagree–but essentially to become involved in a dialogue with the artist. Much of the media is in the first person and, as in any conversation, assumes that the viewer will interact with the work to complete the message. Thus, alternative media usually assumes that the viewer will be an "active" viewer, and challenges the viewer to fulfill that role. Often, there are multiple levels of message and meaning.

The first reaction of most television literate audiences on seeing alternative media is to wonder why the artist didn't "just say it" (although students can often translate their understanding of MTV to watching the more experimental forms of alternative media). A common faculty and administrative reaction is that the subject is not "balanced." Many faculty are hesitant to use it, from an unfamiliarity with the "language" of the medium, a concern about bias, and the resulting desire not to appear "foolish" before their students. Alternative media does alter the traditional relationships between faculty and student. It is the experience of viewing art that creates this change. It creates a peer relationship, as both attempt to find the meanings of the work. Both can bring their opinions into play, as they react to the artist's point of view. Each can learn from the other as they enrich the experience of the work with their own life experiences.

This happened to me while using Valerie Soe's tape *New Year* in a high school in New Jersey. In one part of the tape, the text of a jingle crawls up the screen. "Chinese/Japanese/Dirty knees/Look at these." As we analyzed the media language, one student referred to this poem and the class began to discuss what dirty knees might refer to. One initial suggestion, that it was a child's corruption of "dirty 'nese" brought an immediate response from a student from California, who explained that Asians in that state were often employed as gardeners, and therefore had "dirty knees." (This led us into a discussion of job discrimination, and the stereotypes that arise from that.) Most importantly, for discussions of race and ethnic relationships, alternative media stimulates discussion by providing a focus on someone who is not present: the artist. Where people may be reluctant to speak -- or to speak honestly and freely -- for fear of offending others in the room, the presentation of the artist's point of view allows people to speak the same thoughts by applying them to the work, rather than to each other.

How do I select Alternative Media appropriate to my needs?

The first step is to decide on the theme(s) that you want to address and the outcome that you hope to achieve. Then, you will need to determine the audience composition. Will it be multi-cultural, or limited to members of one community? Does the audience have experience in interacting with members of other race/ethnic groups? Have those experiences been positive or negative? Will the screening take place during a time of intergroup tension, or is the purpose of the screening to prevent such tensions?

Much of alternative media presents multiple layers of meaning; it can be viewed as "narrow-casted" in terms of its coverage. Independent media does not attempt, in many cases, to cover all aspects of an issue. Therefore, the fit between the media, discussion themes, goals of the screening, and audience is important. Once these parameters are clear, it is necessary to determine how you want the media to function in the event. Is the media being used to provoke debate? To stimulate discussion?

To introduce a concept or a racial/ethnic group? Each one of these objectives would require not only a different tape, but may also require different types of work, or the programming of several works.

If the goal is to provoke debate, a highly polarized point of view, or personalized work, could be most appropriate. On the other hand, an autobiographical or dramatic work can stimulate discussion without encouraging debate. In places where intergroup tensions are high, a provocative work could provide a focus for the tensions each side feels, but could equally be divisive. A meditative work could lower tensions enough to allow for discussion. Where the multi-cultural mix of an institution is low, or non-existent, first person works can provide a means of introducing new communities while maintaining a sense of the other's essential humanity.

Much of this body of work is short (20 minutes and under). This allows for such programming options as screening several pieces that present different points of view on the theme (e.g. looking at patriotism from the viewpoint of a an African-American, an Asian, a Native American, and a Caucasian) based on political or ethnic differences. Alternatively, pieces with experimental structures can be combined with documentary work to consider an issue in different ways.

Since alternative media is, by nature, individual in its message and point of view, it is important to be clear about what you hope the audience will get out of it. If you wish to stimulate discussion on defining self-identity, you will need to seek out works that focus on that issue. If you want to explore black experiences in America as a way to explore black/white relationships at your college, you may need to use several pieces to explore the range of experiences blacks have had in this country. The selection of the proper work is critical to developing a good discussion.

The first and most obvious rule in using alternative (or any other form of media) in

discussion is to preview the work. However, selecting alternative media is different from selecting the traditional instructional media. Each piece has to be assessed in terms of its language, point of view, and focus. Often, you will need to preview several pieces before finding the one that works for your goals. Indeed, it often takes several screenings to become completely familiar with some of the work. The preview is also useful in defining how the message is conveyed in the work. Begin your search for alternative media well in advance of your screening dates to allow for relaxed previewing. Because the material can often seem strange structurally, it is difficult to screen a lot of works at one time and remember each one clearly. It may be useful to keep a log with notes.

Sometimes, it is helpful to preview alternative media as a committee or with family or students. Much of this material is created as art work, rather than informational programming, and it can be useful to hear other people's reactions to a work. You should select pieces, after previewing, that you feel some reaction to. If you do not feel in some way affected after previewing a tape or film, then it will be difficult to encourage discussion in a group. However, do not confuse difficulty in articulating reaction ("not having anything to say") with reacting to a piece on levels other than the intellectual. Starting a discussion with "This tape affected me deeply, but I can't quite say why. I do know that I kept thinking about it all week," can be an effective opening. Finally, do not hesitate to program work that you disagree with philosophically; if presented in a non-authoritarian way this can spark good discussions.

Having the catalogs of the distributors of independent media at hand will help to organize the search for programming. Most of these catalogs provide descriptions of the work that will inform you of both the content and structure of each piece. One advantage in using alternative media is that most distributors of independent media want to encourage the use of this media, and will work with you to develop your program if you explain your needs adequately.

How do I start a discussion with Alternative Media?

Any time that alternative media is used, the audience should be informed, through the introduction, if the work that they will see is not of a familiar instructional or television form. It is important to let them know the primary reason why the work is being screened -- that is, why you selected this piece -- to ensure that the following discussion can be focused. It is often useful to tell them something about how the audio and visuals are integrated, though without describing the entire work. Most importantly, the audience should know that they will be viewing art. Therefore, there are no right and wrong answers, but there are opinions, experiences, and imagination for them to draw upon in responding to work. The work is one person's opinion -- the audience is entitled to have theirs.

The discussion should follow immediately after the screening, while the work is clear in the minds of the audience. Explain to the audience how the discussion will be structured in advance -- and be prepared to abandon your game plan if it becomes clear that the audience is moving in a different direction that is equally as useful and valid. Many of these works can be "read" on several levels depending on the experiences of the audience.

When presenting alternative media in discussion contexts, I have often found that to begin by analyzing the media language (the visuals, audio, and how they are combined) is the best way to get the audience to discuss the meaning and the larger issues addressed in the work. There are several reasons for this. First, it allows the audience to overcome their hesitancy about confronting each other by maintaining a focus on the artist's statement, rather than each others' opinions.

Secondly, it allows students to become more at ease with the form of the work, thus encouraging dialogue. Third, it helps the audience to distinguish the multiple layers of meaning in the work. In doing an analysis of the media language, I find it useful to log the counter numbers of particularly important sections, so they can be replayed during the discussion (a function much easier in video than in film). Replays can be done without the sound or without the picture to focus attention on a given part of the piece. It is a simple step in this type of analysis from asking "How else could the artist have said this?" to "How would you have said this if you were the artist?" to "Would that actually say the same thing the artist said?"

How do I analyze the media language?

There are many approaches to analyzing film and video language; however, there is no one way that is right for every work. The formal structures of this work can vary from the traditional documentary to the most experimental video art. Therefore, I will give some general guidelines.

In general, analyzing media language as a way to raise discussion of larger issues depends on starting the discussion context at the very beginning. Therefore, raise questions--don't define for the audience what a work "means." Encourage alternative interpretations of the text. Be prepared not to defend your interpretation, but to share the process by which you arrived at it.

Avoid general questions (What is the point of this work?) at the beginning. These often elicit little, if any, response. It is often a better strategy to begin with focused questions on the content (Did anyone else get a sense of disappointment from this work? Disappointment about what?) or the form (Why do you think that the artist shows us Marilyn Monroe under a poem about equality? What was she saying about her image?). Another technique to initiate the discussion is to replay a specific segment of the work and to ask the audience to pay particular attention to the relationship of the sound to the image or of one image to another. Following the replay, ask the audience to explain why they thought the artist arranged things that way, what alternative arrangements might exist, and whether the meaning would have changed if the alternative was chosen.

As the discussion builds, and the audience becomes more comfortable, you can begin to ask how they would have created a similar statement. This encourages them to consider the decisions the artist made about what to show, and what to edit out. By filling in the gaps of the statement, the discussion can be directed towards the larger issues. This is a good point to include role-playing as a dynamic in the discussion. A white student can respond about how they would have created a statement on being the "other" using the artist's statement as a guide, and imagination as the filler. Role-playing can also help to expose the stereotypes and misconceptions that exist in the audience's understanding of the community the work represents.

Analyzing the media language is useful to initiate discussion, but can be abandoned as soon as it becomes clear that the audience wants to move onto a discussion of the larger issues. However, the use of media language analysis can be re-introduced to shift the discussion to other issues in the work. When programming several works at the same event, it is my experience that the discussion works best if held after all the works have been screened. In this case, the analysis of the media language can be used as a way to encourage a comparison of the different works, particularly in how the artists' statements both agree and disagree. Audiences can often become confused between the works, and the use of replay of segments helps to distinguish each work.

Media Analysis

The example of media analysis which follows is based on a one and one-half minute section of an experimental narrative work called *FLAG*. The tape explores, in a semi-autobiographical form, patriotism from an African-American woman's point of view. The tape has two performers: a white artist, representing the videomaker's diary Heidi, who makes American flags in a variety of media; and a black dancer, representing the videomaker, who performs with the artist's flags. The tape is divided into three sections, *Childhood, Adolescence*, and *The Present*. In the videotape, images and text are repeated in different forms and/ or contexts to explore how their meanings change.

The section analyzed here is from close to the middle of the Adolescence section of *FLAG*. When working with this section, I focus the discussion on three points: the reinterpretation of the meaning of symbols, the changing emotions of the protagonist, and the shift of the work's focus from the social to the personal.

I begin by focusing the discussion on the visuals by replaying the section without the audio. Then, I ask the audience to list the key image motifs of the section. In most cases, the audience notes without prompting that many of these motifs are variants of the motif as originally seen in *Childhood* or the beginning of *Adolescence*. The visual motifs commonly mentioned are:

1. The Salutes--the gestures out-of-sync. This motif is originally seen in the *Childhood* section under a collage of Girl Scout pledge/Brownie pledge/Pledge of Allegiance, with the performers saluting in sync. In discussion, the focus is on why the performers are now "out-of-sync."

2. Kissing--this motif is originally seen at the beginning of *Adolescence*. Points raised about this image include racism in attaching

CROWD CHANT
"The people united will never be defeated."
(repeated 3 times)

NARRATOR
All men are created equal.

NARRATOR
The concept of all men are created equal
is important to Americans.

MUSIC

"weight" to physical characteristics, and the impact of adolescence upon social relationships.

3. Marilyn Monroe Portrait w/Artist's Portrait inserted -- this image often gets a "chuckle" from the audience, and the reaction is used to begin the discussion. The discussion topics included social concepts of beauty and their personal impact.

4. Marilyn Monroe Portrait with "Embarrassed" Performer American Flag, with "Embarrassed" Performer Slave Ship, with "Embarrassed" Performer--this is a point when the audience often becomes very quiet. The discussion revolves around "What is the performer ashamed or angry about?" and "How does the underlying image effect how we interpret the emotion and its focus?" It is also noted that this is the first time the performer reacts directly to the audience as an individual.

On the second replay of the segment, I include the audio track. It usually requires little prompting to initiate a discussion on how the audio/text impacts on our understanding of the meanings of the visual motifs and of the segment. When the audio/text is played, audiences seem to shift the discussion from the person to American ideals and how their meaning can change depending on personal experience. The strategy I often use is to have the audience consider the relationship between the visuals and the audio, and how the meaning of the audio would change if the context did. I encourage the audience to verbalize how their interpretation of the images alone changes. For example:

1. The Salute/Out of Sync with Chant--*Out of Sync* is often described in terms of the race of the performers when the visuals are presented alone. When the audio is added, the social context of the 1960s (and people's varied relationships to the government) becomes a factor in interpreting individual behavior.

2. Marilyn Monroe with Artist's Portrait--When the essay on the phrase "All Men are Created Equal" is added to the image, the questions raised by the "weight" of racism extend beyond the personal to the possibility that the American ideals are also empty.

3. Slave Ship with "Embarrassed" Performer-- The ending of the essay, "but who says they die that way?" provides a focus for the dancer's emotions that brings both a historical and a political dimension to this image. It urges a reconsideration of American ideals in light of the history of our actual behavior, and it points to possible political positions that the individual could adopt.

In discussions of this style, the focus is on how our understanding of the work is enhanced by each layer of image and audio. Thus, the responses that develop when considering the images are not subsequently found to be "wrong," but are further developed when the audio/text is added. In this work, the meanings can be read simultaneously on both personal and social levels.

A discussion of this type is both more fluid and less time-consuming than the preceding written example would lead one to believe. Audiences often will anticipate the direction of the discussion: for example, moving directly into a discussion of the image with the audio. The facilitator can allow the audience to develop the discussion at its own pace.

NARRATOR
Maybe all men are created equal, but who says they die that way?

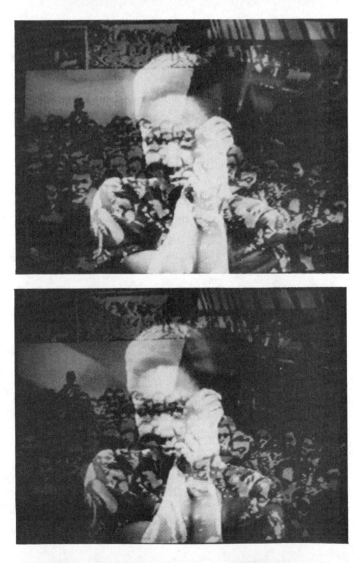

SELECTED FILM AND VIDEOTAPES

**You May
Want to Obtain**

recommended
by Linda
Gibson

All Orientals Look the Same
Directed by Valerie Soe
Contact: Women Make Movies
1986 Original Format: Video 1:30
Staking a claim for diversity through a juxtaposition of faces and Asian ethnicities confronting the viewer with the title phrase.

An I for an I
Directed by Lawrence Andrews
Contact: The Video Data Bank
1988 Original Format: Video 18:00
In this artist's plea, the production of violence in culture and media causes a struggling and violent reaction.

Black Celebration
Directed by Tony Cokes
Contact: The Video Data Bank
1988 Original Format: Video 17:00
This engaged reading of the 60's black riots reads them as a refusal to participate in the logic of capital and an attempt to de-fetishize the commodity through theft and gift.

Bombs Aren't Cool!
Directed by Joan Jubela and Stan Davis
Contact: First Run Icarus Films
1986 Original Format: Video 5:00
A music video that raps to young people about the perils of nuclear war and militarism, featuring rap masters, *The Deuce*.

Coffee Colored Children
Directed by Ngozi A. Onwurah
Contact: Women Make Movies
1988 Original Format: Film 15:00
Recollections of growing up the only mixed-race (Black/White) children in an English town create a testimony to the profound internalized effects of racism and the struggle for pride.

Color Schemes
Directed by Shu Lea Cheang
Contact: The Video Data Bank
1989 Original Format: Video 28:40
A multi-layered discourse on racism and assimilation that condemns the former and refuses to condone the latter, using the washing machine as a metaphor for the American "melting pot."

FLAG
Directed by Linda Gibson
Contact: Women Make Movies
1989 Original Format: Video 24:00
The history, identity and significance of the videomaker is seen through her relationship to the iconography of the American flag.

Family Gathering
Directed by Lise Yasui
Contact: New Day Films
1988 Original Format: Film 30:00
A personal look at the Japanese internment and the repercussions of those events, myths, memories, and silences surrounding Yasui's family history.

From Here, From This Side
Directed by Gloria Ribe
Contact: Women Make Movies
1988 Original Format: Video 24:00
This collage-like documentary forces U.S. American viewers to consider the question of cultural imperialism from "the other side."

Inside Life Outside
Directed by Sachiko Hamada and Scott Sinkler
Contact: New Day Films
1988 Original Format: Video 57:00
A cinema verite study of a group of homeless people living in shantytown in the Lower East Side of New York creates a powerful and intimate look into the world of the homeless.

La Ofrenda: Day of the Dead
Directed by Lourdes Portillo and Susana Munoz
Contact: Lourdes Portillo
1989 Original Format: Film 50:00
A personal look at the loving, sometimes humorous, Mexican and Chicano attitudes towards death.

Machito: A Latin Jazz Legacy
Directed by Carlos Ortiz
Contact: First Run Icarus Films
1987 Original Format: Film 58:00
A portrait of Frank "Machito" Grillo, who has become synonymous with Latin Jazz, that weaves together vintage film clips and recordings, street performances, and interviews.

Meta Mayan II
Directed by Edin Velez
Contact: Electronic Arts Intermix
1981 Original Format: Video 20:00
Shot in the Guatemalan highlands, Meta Mayan is a keenly observed poetic video essay on the indigenous culture of the Mayan Indians.

New Year, Parts I and II
Directed by Valerie Soe
Contact: Women Make Movies
1988 Original Format: Video 20:00
The memory of Chinese heritage in America, seen through storybook drawings and the experience of the world through racist media images.

Picking Tribes
Directed by Saundra Sharp
Contact: Women Make Movies
1988 Original Format: Film 7:00
A light look at a daughter of the 40's as she struggles to find an identity between her Black and Native American heritages.

Racism: 101
Directed by Tom Lennon for Frontline
Contact: Frontline
1988 Original: Video 58:00
This investigation of racist incidents and anti-racist activism in American universities offers perspectives from black and white students and faculty about the persistence of racism.

Reflections
Directed by Kim Watson and Caleb Oglesby
Contact: Third World Newsreel
1987 Original Format: Video 6:00
The voice and vision of Dr. Martin Luther King, Jr. provide a "reflection" on the history and implications of the civil rights movement.

Salaam Bombay
Directed by Mira Nair
Contact: Cinecom
1988 Original Format: Film 114:50
An evocative portrait of a young boy's life on the streets of Bombay, presented with sadness, humor, and a ray of hope.

Sun, Moon & Feather
Directed by Bob Rosen and Jane Zipp
Contact: Cinema Guild
1989 Original Format: Film 30:00
The life of three Native American sisters growing up in 1930s Brooklyn, featuring the Spiderwoman Theatre.

Surname Viet Given Name Nam
Directed by Trinh T. Minh Ha
Contact: Women Make Movies
1989 Original Format: Film 108:00
A profoundly personal documentary that challenges official culture with the voices of women, using dance, printed texts, folk poetry, and the words of North and South Vietnamese women.

The Civil Rights Rap Video
Produced by Richard Delaura, Peter Ladue and Thom Thacker
Contact: Rapping Up History
1987 Original Format: Video 6:00
Boston teenagers relate the major chapters of the civil rights struggle of the late 1950s and 1960s, through a multi-verse explanation of Brown vs. Board of Ed., Rosa Parks, etc.

The Displaced View
Directed by Midi Ohodena
Contact: Women Make Movies
1988 Original Format: Film 52:00
A granddaughter's search for identity within the history of Japanese in North America, woven of experimental, dramatic, and documentary forms creates a love letter to the family's women.

Unfinished Diary
Directed by Marilu Mallet
Contact: Women Make Movies
1986 Original Format: Film 55:00
A powerful film about language, gender, exile and immigration, this semi-autobiographical docu-drama explores the profound cultural silences of a Chilean emigre in French Canada.

Major Distributors of Alternative Media on Topics of Race and Ethnic Relations

African Diaspora Images
PO Box 3517
Brooklyn, NY 11201
718-852-8353

Black Filmmaker Foundation
80 8th Avenue # 1704
New York, NY 10011
212-924-1198

California Newsreel
149 9th St. #420
San Francisco, CA 94103
415-621-6196

Cinecom
1250 Broadway
New York, NY 10001
212-239-8360

The Cinema Guild
1697 Broadway
New York, NY 10019
212-246-5522

Electronic Arts Intermix
536 Broadway, 9th Floor
New York, NY 10012
212-966-4605

First Run Icarus Films
153 Waverly Pl. 6th Floor
New York, NY 10014
212-727-1711

Frontline
225 W. 26th St.
New York, NY 10001

Intermedia Arts Minnesota
425 Ontario St. SE
Minneapolis, MN 55414
612-627-4444

Lourdes Portillo
981 Esmeradla St.
San Francisco, CA
415-824-5850

Na Maka o ka 'Aina
2460-D Waolani Ave.
Honolulu, Hawaii 96817
808-595-7728

National Asian American Telecommunications Consortium
346 Ninth St. 2nd Floor
San Francisco, CA 94103
415-863-0814

New Day Films
853 Broadway Suite 1210
New York, NY 10003
212-477-4604

Rappin Up History
2 Speridakis Terrace
Cambridge, MA 02139

Third World Newsreel
335 W. 38th St. 5th Floor
New York, NY 10018
212-947-9277

The Video Data Bank
37 S. Wabash
Chicago, IL 60603
312-443-3793

Visual Communications
2630 S. Los Angeles Ave. #307
Los Angeles, CA 90012
213-680-4462

Women Make Movies
225 Lafayette St., Ste.211
New York, NY 10012
212-925-0606

Black Student Retention in Higher Education: What We Have Learned

ABOUT THE AUTHOR:

Dr. Clinita Ford

Dr. Clinita Ford is professor of Academic Affairs and director of Title III Programs at Florida A&M University in Tallahassee, Florida. She is also the founder and director of the *National Conference on Black Student Retention in Higher Education*, which has been held annually since 1985. She received her B.S. degree from Lincoln University in Missouri, her M.S. from Columbia University in Vocational Home Economics education, and her Ph.D. in Nutrition and Biochemistry from Kansas State University.

Dr. Ford has established a distinguished career that has earned her many awards and honors. She has been noted in *Who's Who in American*

Education, Who's Who of American Women, Outstanding Educators of America, Outstanding Personalities of the South, and *American Men and Women of Science.* Other honors and awards include the Distinguished Alumni Award from Kansas State University (1970), the Alumni Achievement Award from Lincoln University (1968), Teacher of the Year Award from Florida A&M University (1966), and the Distinguished Alumni Award from the National Association for Equal Opportunity in Higher Education in 1989. Dr. Ford is a noted lecturer and consultant on minority retention in higher education.

ABOUT THE AUTHOR:

Dr. Marvel
Lang

Dr. Marvel Lang is a native of Mississippi, where he earned his B.A. from Jackson State University in 1970. He received his M.A. from the University of Pittsburgh in 1975; and a Ph.D. with a specialty in Urban/Social and Economic Geography, Rural Settlement, and Quantitative methods with computer applications, from Michigan State University in 1979. He has been director of the Center for Urban Affairs and Associate Professor at Michigan State since 1986. His experience includes research and analysis of states' policies and regulations on nuclear waste and hazardous waste disposal, the impacts of the restrictive energy economy on families during the 1970s, and he has directed numerous other research efforts.

Currently, Dr. Lang is involved in a project to develop and test alternative criteria for defining urban and rural populations for the U.S. census. Also, his current research involves a study of urban development processes and patterns in less developed countries, intended to revise the parameters of urban development theory. Dr. Lang has held previous positions at Jackson State University and the U.S. Census Bureau in Washington, D.C.

INTRODUCTION

By the year 2000, one-third of all school-aged children and 42 percent of public school enrollments will be minorities. Retaining these students in the educational system until high school, or if they continue, college graduation, is a big challenge. Attrition rates of minority students in American colleges and universities are currently atrocious. This article presents the historical background necessary to understand the magnitude of the retention problem, patterns of African-American post-high school education, and compares those patterns at predominately white and black campuses.

The factors that contribute to the high attrition rates of black students are examined in depth. These include:

> The normative problems of black students;
> Institutional circumstances that promote student retention or create barriers to minority student access; and
> Changing sociologies and political economies of higher education.

The authors issue a plea to educational institutions to implement what is already known about furthering retention of minority students. They cite a mandate to department heads and deans at Wright State University in Dayton, Ohio, to increase the numbers of minority faculty as rare evidence of the type of action that is needed. At that university, compliance with the mandate is tied to departmental budgets and personnel merit increases, a strategy that the authors endorse.

The authors suggest that what we have learned to date about Black student retention is sufficient knowledge to guide the implementation of reasonable and feasible institutional and societal solutions to the problems.

BLACK STUDENT RETENTION IN HIGHER EDUCATION:

What we Have Learned

by
Clinita A. Ford
Marvel Lang

During the past six years there has been a wealth of research, writings, conferences, national attention, and genuine public concern about the problems and issues related to black student retention in higher education institutions in the United States. This concern and attention was brought about in the early 1980s when it was realized that the gains that had been made by blacks in achieving access and success in higher education were being lost. The reasons for this reversal were:

(a) high and increasing rates of attrition and dropouts,

(b) declining black enrollments in 4-year colleges and universities,

(c) faltering enrollments and graduation by blacks in graduate and professional schools, and

(d) a generally changing climate, environment, and attitude toward blacks in terms of access, admissions and recruitment to institutions of higher learning.

Recently, the attention and concern about black student retention has been heightened by the release of new data and projections on the future of the American population's demographic structure and the future workforce. For example, it has been predicted and projected that by the year 2020, one-third of our nation's population will be blacks and other minorities (American Council on Education, 1988). It is further projected that by the year 2000, an increasingly larger proportion of those youths seeking to enter college will be minorities (U.S. Department of Education, 1988). Why are these predictions valid? Today, all of the people who will enter college in the year 2000, all of those who will be 65 years of age in the year 2020, and all those who will be 65 years of age in the year 2051 have already been born. Thus, if we examine the demographic structure of the current population, coupled with the reproductive patterns and trends of that population, combining these with reasonable projection models, we can easily derive some solid indications of our demographic future.

Given what we already know, it has been projected that by the year 2000, one-third of all school-aged children and 42 percent of public school enrollments will be minorities. This scenario presents a significant challenge to our total society. That challenge is to seriously address the problem of educating minorities to become gainfully and productively employed citizens who will contribute to the general welfare of the society rather than be a burden on the public welfare of the nation. Considering the already known future of the workworld, adequate education for the future labor force will indubitably mean a college education for many. The problem becomes that of getting minority students through high school and into college, and retaining them through graduation. Retention becomes a crucial ingredient in the solution to this problem.

The significance of black student retention in higher education has only recently gained national prominence, especially over the past six or seven years. Nevertheless, the magnitude of this problem has been such that it has commanded widespread attention. Both the research and writings on the subject have been voluminous. Our purpose in this chapter is to summarize what we have learned about black student retention in higher education as a result of these efforts from practical, conceptual/ theoretical, and programmatic perspectives. The ultimate objective is to assess if what we have learned already is sufficient knowledge to guide the implementation of reasonable and feasible institutional and societal solutions to the problems.

The Status of Blacks in Higher Education

One thing we have learned emphatically over the past five years is that the status of blacks in higher education has begun to decline relative to the gains that were made from the mid-1960s to the mid-1970s. For example, between 1976-77 and 1984-85, the number of blacks enrolled in graduate schools decreased by 12,518, or 19.2 percent. Thus, the black percentage of total graduate school enrollment in 1984 was only 4.8 percent compared to 6 percent of the total in 1976. In 1985, only 909 black Americans received Ph.D. degrees compared to 20,641 whites (Lang, 1988; U.S. Census Bureau, 1985). This scenario was occurring at the same time that the number of blacks enrolled in undergraduate colleges across the country had increased from 665,000 in 1975 to 786,000 in 1984. Nevertheless, the percentage of total black high school graduates who enrolled in college had decreased from 32 percent in 1975 to 27.2 percent in 1984.

Thus, we have learned that a significant component of the retention problem is getting black youths from high school into college. Another significant component of the problem is keeping them in college through graduation, not to mention improving their access to graduate and professional schools.

In 1984, there were nearly 40,000 fewer blacks enrolled in college than in 1976, although during that period college enrollments in general continued to rise and the enrollments of other minority students rose significantly (Christoffel, 1986; Lang, 1990b, forthcoming). For example, between 1980 and 1985 college enrollment increased by only approximately 100,000, from 12.1 million to 12.2 million. While the overall proportion of minority students in colleges increased from 15.4 percent to 17 percent between 1976 and 1987, the proportion of blacks in colleges fell from 9.4 percent to 8.8 percent during the same period (Center for Education Statistics, 1987). Much of this decline was attributed to the decreasing number of black males enrolling in college (Lang, 1988).

Still, substantial gains have been made over the past two decades in the total educational status of blacks, especially beyond the secondary level. In 1970, for example, blacks constituted 7 percent of total college enrollments; by 1980 this proportion had increased to 11 percent, but had fallen to 8.8 percent by 1987 (Matney & Johnson, 1983; Allen, 1987). Similarly, in 1970, only 31 percent of blacks 25 years of age and over were at least high school graduates compared to 51 percent in 1980. By 1980, eight percent of blacks had completed four or more years of college, compared to only four percent ten years earlier in 1970 (U.S. Bureau of the Census, 1987).

Nevertheless, the proportion of blacks earning college degrees, compared to the proportion of whites earning college degrees, has decreased significantly during the 1970 to 1980 decade at all levels and in all types of institutions. Between 1981-82 and 1984-85, even at predominantly black institutions, degrees conferred to black students increased at the sub-baccalaureate, doctoral, and first professional degree levels; but declined at the bachelors and masters degree levels. Consequently, the numbers of blacks enrolled in graduate schools decreased by 12,518, or 19.2 percent between 1976-77 and 1984-85 (Lang, 1990a, Forthcoming). Based on what we know from recent national reports, it can be stated rather assuredly that these trends have continued over the past five years.

When we examine the recent patterns of black student enrollment in colleges, the picture is one of dismal decline and rapid attrition. In 1977, fifty percent of all black high school graduates enrolled in college compared to 51 percent for whites; 1977 was the peak year for black college enrollments. By 1981, this figure had fallen to 40 percent, and by 1982 it had fallen again to 36 percent. Thus, in 1985 the percentage of blacks 18 to 25 years of age who were enrolled in college was 26.1 percent; down from 33.5 percent for this age cohort in 1976 (Lang, 1988b).

It is clear that the overall status of blacks in the higher education arena has worsened during the 1980s decade, after reaching its highest levels in the 1970s. What is surprising and somewhat alarming is the fact that this situation is as true for predominantly black institutions--the traditional mainstay for blacks' post-secondary degrees--as for predominantly white institutions where attrition rates for blacks have always been atrociously high. Until the late 1960s, most of the growth in college enrollment took place at predominantly black institutions. In the late 1970s, this momentum in college enrollment growth shifted to white institutions after black enrollments peaked in the mid to late 1970s. In 1973, for example, 85 black colleges enrolled 42 percent of all blacks attending college and granted 70 percent of the bachelors degrees awarded to blacks. Today, although black colleges enroll only approximately 16 percent of black students attending college, they still award over two-thirds of the undergraduate degrees earned by blacks (Wharton, 1986; Lang, 1986; Fleming, 1984).

Hence, we have learned that between 1977, when black college enrollments peaked, and 1989, something has happened to reverse the trend of progress that occurred between 1960 and 1977. The voluminous research of the past few years has provided excellent insights into the various factors that have effectuated this reversal. We shall turn now to discuss those factors.

Summarily, the factors that contribute to high attrition rates of black students in higher education can be classified into several categories as follows:

1. **The normative problems of black students.** A set of factors that are:

   (a) the result of black students' socioeconomic backgrounds and families,

   (b) their secondary schooling and preparation for college,

   (c) their socialization and coping skills, and

   (d) attitudes, behavioral patterns, self-discipline, self-motivation, etc.

2. **Institutional circumstances that promote minority student retention or create barriers to minority student access.**

   These are factors that exist at institutions that either serve to promote the access and retention of minority students generally, or serve to deter their retention. These may include:

   (a) institutionalized retention programs,

   (b) advising and counseling,

   (c) mentoring programs and minority faculty role models,

   (d) recruitment and admissions policies, and

   (e) financial and human resources, etc.

3. **The changing sociologies and political economies of higher education.**

   These are factors that derive from changing policymaking and public policy perspectives at the federal and state levels, and the changing patterns, processes and norms that institutions of higher learning adopt in order to adapt to the changes which affect the sociology and group dynamics at the institutions.

The normative problems of Black students

Without a doubt, the majority of black students who enroll in college come with a set of factors that will either directly or indirectly impinge on their achievement. Likewise, they will face a set of circumstances at college that will automatically affect their success as well. The realization of these facts have taught us that black student retention in college, as well as that of all students, must begin not when they enter college, but in kindergarten and continue through high school.

We have learned that the problems of black student retention and attrition in higher education cannot be divorced from their sociocultural, socioeconomic, and family backgrounds; or the ramifications of the larger society that perpetuates these factors. Specifically, the research over the past few years has shown overwhelmingly that a large majority of black students who come to college are ill-prepared either academically, financially, or emotionally to deal with the rigors of college life. It has also been documented that the majority of black students who drop out of predominantly white institutions do so not because they are academically or intellectually incapable, but for other reasons (Lang, 1988a).

Minority students in general, and most black youths in particular, are getting a raw deal in the American education system. This is especially true in those areas where black parents neither have the resources, the background, nor the political savvy to assure that the systems are providing the best possible educational opportunity for their children. In areas throughout the country where blacks live and are in the majority, the conditions for learning and the quality of education in the schools in their communities are inherently lower on every known indicator of quality. Since the 1970s, inner-city schools in almost every major metropolitan area of the country have become populated predominantly by blacks or some other ethnic minority. Similarly, it has been shown that 64 percent of the nation's poor live in impoverished areas of the 100 largest cities (Ascher, 1987) and many of these are blacks (Lang, 1990b, forthcoming).

How do these circumstances translate into poor quality education? Overwhelmingly these minority/black dominated schools are still controlled both politically and administratively by whites. Thus, several of the main ingredients of poor educational quality are consistently present in school districts where minority youths constitute the majority of the schools' populations. Those factors include:

(a) more overcrowded classrooms,

(b) teachers with fewer advanced degrees and credentials,

(c) less resources and personnel for counseling,

(d) few, if any, role models of the same race or ethnic background, and

(e) less opportunities for enrichment and exposure to enriching activities outside the classroom (Orfield & Paul, 1988).

Hence, students from such school environments have a decided learning and achievement disadvantage.

The problems for black college youths, who overwhelmingly come from the American public school system at the secondary level, are amplified only because they get the worst of "a system seethed in mediocrity," a term coined by the National Commission on Excellence in Education (NCEE). The Commission notes:

1. Some 23 million American adults are functionally illiterate.

2. About 13 percent of all 17 year olds can be considered functionally illiterate.

3. Functional illiteracy among minority youth 17 years of age may run as high as 40 percent.

4. Average achievement of high school students on most standardized tests is now lower than 26 years ago (NCEE, 1983).

Though the problem of academic unpreparedness for college is not necessarily their own doing in many instances, black college students are blamed for this failure in the system and become the victims; they are penalized by being denied access to many of the better institutions, and upon entering college, by the additional burden of developmental and remedial program requirements. Yet, few researchers, college administrators, or faculty members for that matter will acknowledge that these problems are as much the fault of the white-dominated public school systems from which these students come as they are the results of their deprived and impoverished family backgrounds from which an overwhelming majority of them

come. It is ludicrous for us to expect students who come from families whose total household income averages between $15,000 and $20,000 per year, and who must attend the admittedly poorest schools, to perform on the same levels as those whose families' incomes average over $35,000 a year and who attend the best secondary schools (Lang, 1986).

On the other hand, too many black students come to college lacking too many of the proper socialization, coping, and behavioral adjustment skills needed to be able to compete successfully. Tinto (1975) has pointed out that academic failure or success may be viewed as a longitudinal process of interactions between the individual and the academic and social systems of the institution. Thus, the experiences of a student in a particular academic setting are continually modifying his or her goals and institutional commitments in such ways that will either lead to positive motivation to persist and succeed, or to negative motivation, attitudes, and eventual discontinuance and failure--dropout.

Regarding the circumstances of black students, this literally translates into the fact that because of their particular family and secondary schooling backgrounds, too many enter college lacking certain necessary attributes. These consist of:

(a) academic abilities and skills,

(b) coping and social adjustment skills,

(c) self-discipline and time management skills,

(d) appropriate study habits, self-motivation, and

(e) other factors that have strong relationships and predictive influence on their successful achievement in the academic setting at the higher education level (Lang, 1988; Stamps, 1985; Tinto, 1975).

Institutional circumstances and barriers

The research on black student retention in higher education in recent years has not only elucidated the problems of students; but has also shown forth the barriers to minority student access and retention inherent in the institutions themselves. For certain, it has become clear that the preparation for retention and success in college must begin at the elementary school level if not at the preschool/kindergarten level. Nevertheless, knowing the deteriorating situation of most public school systems across the country, there are things that colleges and universities could do better that are not being done at all. Plus, there are attitudes and philosophies that are prevalent at institutions that are antiquated and irrelevant to our contemporary societal needs.

The Civil Rights movement of the 1950s to the 1970s was as much a struggle to gain for minorities, and especially blacks, the right to equal access to educational opportunities at the nation's institutions of higher learning, as it was to gain equal access to its lunch counters. Still, three and one-half decades after *Brown vs. the Board of Education*, blacks and other minorities are despairingly underrepresented at these institutions both as students and as faculty and staff, especially at predominantly white institutions. Although the access of other minorities has increased generally, the access of black students specifically has absolutely declined over the 1980's decade.

Nominally, the problems of blacks in higher education are increasingly those of access and retention. While institutions boast vehemently about their growing enrollments of blacks annually, they try as vehemently to disguise the higher rates of attrition (dropouts), the pitiful low rates of graduation, and the declining enrollment of blacks in graduate and professional schools.

Previous research on minority access and retention has substantially documented the main factors that contribute to the current trends. These factors include:

1. The ingrained institutional racism which both denies blacks admission and stymies their motivation, self-esteem, and confidence to compete at predominantly white institutions.

2. The lack of necessary counseling, advising, nurturing, mentoring, and ethnically identifiable role models.

3. The lack of available institutional financial resources for support and the intensifying competition for these resources.

4. The lack of institutional commitment to equal opportunity and affirmative action.

5. Increasing college costs relative to black families' incomes and resources.

There is no doubt that institutional racism persists and is a major contributor to the declining enrollment and increasing dropout rates of blacks in colleges.

During the 1980s, when the Reagan Administration spurned affirmative action policies and civil rights generally, predominantly white colleges and universities used the administration's rhetoric as their signal to abandon efforts to increase equal access for blacks (Wilson, 1989). The flood of racist incidents on campuses in recent years attests to this fact, as does the leveling and recent decline of hiring efforts aimed at increasing the numbers of blacks as faculty and administrators. Astin (1982) found blacks significantly underrepresented at 56 out of 65 of the flagship universities in the country, and Hispanics underrepresented at 49 out of the same institutions. Recent findings by Pruitt (1989) show that these circumstances have worsened generally rather than improved.

In 1988, of the 18,500 full-time black faculty members at colleges and universities across the country, 8,000 were employed at black institutions, comprising 68 percent of their faculties. Comparatively, the 10,600 black faculty at white institutions account for a mere 2.3 percent of the total full-time faculty members (Maguire, 1988). This situation, especially at the white institutions, has grave impacts and consequences regarding the success of black students. The presence of black faculty to serve as mentors and role models for black students has tremendous impact on black students at white colleges. Comparative statistics have shown that the success rate of black students at these institutions is directly related to the numbers of black faculty and staff (Fleming, 1984; Gavin, 1989).

Also, during the 1980s most institutions have experienced tremendous cutbacks in the resources available from federal programs for student financial support. Many institutions have used this situation to justify the reduction of their efforts to recruit and enroll minority students. Invariably a larger proportion of black students rely on some form of financial aid to support their college education because of the general inferior socioeconomic status of most black families. Coupled with the constantly rising cost of college tuition and other expenses as well as tighter restrictions on financial aid awards, a large proportion of black students have been priced out of the higher education market regardless of their academic capabilities. Likewise, the number of black students who drop out of college because of the lack of adequate financial resources has almost doubled during the last five years. Institutions generally have not done much to alleviate this situation.

The lack of institutional commitment to equal educational opportunity for blacks, the insensitivity of faculty, and subtle racism on the part of faculty and staff shows up in the classroom and in grading and evaluation of black students. These factors are much harder to document and thus harder to address. Even worse, while institutions recognize the horrid academic situations at inner-city public schools from which many black students come, instead of considering better criteria on which to evaluate them for admission, they have sought to make the traditional criteria (standardized test scores) more rigorous in recent years. Usually these racist attitudes and acts are disguised with the argument that implementing different admission criteria will "lower the quality" or "tarnish the image" of the institution.

Considering the academic backgrounds from which many black students come, there is a recognized need for colleges to devise both new criteria by which to predict their success in college and to devise counseling and advising programs to help them map their paths through the academic and bureaucratic maze. But institutions look upon developmental and remediation programs, or any other programs that will address the specific needs of underprepared students (many of whom are not minorities or blacks) as automatically lowering their standards. In these days of fiscal constraints and budget reductions at many institutions, they are not providing these essential services adequately for the majority students. As academic institutions are microcosms of the larger society, they reflect the prevailing attitudes and demeanors of the larger society. In most instances, practices and traditions at these institutions are much harder to change than they are in the larger society.

Practitioners in higher education know that action at higher education institutions permeates from the top down. Thus, if the boards of trustees and chief academic officers at these institutions were to commit themselves to equal opportunity and direct their subordinates to carry out the mandate, minority access and success in colleges would improve dramatically and within due time. But Orfield and Paul (1988) have appropriately characterized the present situation regarding the access and retention of blacks in higher education when they state that "where there is no commitment there can be only token response or none at all" (p. 61).

The changing sociologies and political economics of Higher Education

The changing public policy and group dynamics in the American society during the past decade have transcended into the sociologies and political economics of higher education institutions. Hence, what we see occurring in the larger society is reflected in the academy which is a microcosm of the larger society and its politics.

We know that past federal programs and policies did much to improve the access and the lot of minorities, especially blacks, in higher education. It was during the administration of President John F. Kennedy that significant policies were initiated for the provision of federal resources to aid minority students' access and pursuit of a college education. During the early 1960s, the federal government instituted and appropriated such programs as the National Defense Education Act (NDEA), the National Defense Student Loan Programs (NDSL) and other work-study programs that made it possible for minority students to have the financial support necessary to attend college en-masse for the first time in the nation's history. These were followed by the Civil Rights Laws of the mid-1960s and U.S. Supreme Court rulings that mandated the admission of blacks at predominantly white institutions.

In the late 1960s and early 1970s other federal programs were instituted that increased minority access and prompted the peak period of black college enrollment in the late 1970s. These programs included Basic Education Opportunity Grants Program (BEOG) and the Equal Education Opportunity Program (EEOP), both of which provided direct loans or grants to minority students who qualified for college admission and enrollment.

Under the Reagan Administration, substantial reallocations were made in federal education and student financial aid programs. These reallocations have had significant impacts on minority access to higher education, especially on black students who overwhelmingly and disproportionately depended on these programs to finance their college education. In recent years, significantly larger numbers of black students have had to drop out of college because of a lack of financial resources.

Taking their cues from the federal government's actions and rhetoric, academic institutions have used this era of fiscal conservatism at both the federal and state levels to return to a lackadaisical attitude regarding initiatives to recruit and retain minority students and faculty. Still, while policymaking at the federal level would send a positive signal, policymaking and legislation alone, as we have seen in the past, do not change attitudes and commitment. It is attitudes and commitments as well as leadership at institutions that must change before the principles and practices of affirmative action and equal educational opportunity become more than inscriptions at the bottom of institutional stationery.

In lieu of new legislation and policymaking, the lack of enforcement of existing laws and regulations by appropriate authorities at both the state and federal levels have sent the message to institutions that they can be lax in affirmative action and equal opportunities; both in hiring faculty and staff, and in recruiting and admitting students. The laxness that has come about is being played out by recent administrative maneuvers and grandiose schemes at institutions which are merely smoke screens of rhetoric without any significant dollars or human resources being allocated to ensure any significant impacts on the institution.

This is the nature of the new sociologies that are being brought about at institutions. While the numbers of blacks being recruited and admitted are diminishing rapidly, and the hiring of new black faculty has reached a net zero sum, institutional administrators are rhetorically calling for "more research" and concocting grandiose schemes, both of which serve to forestall actual progress in recruitment and retention of minorities. The fact of the matter is we already know more than enough to solve the problem. Mainly what is needed is direct action and definitive commitment with appropriate administrative actions, if the mandates for action are not carried out at the college and department levels.

For example, Michigan State University during the 1988-89 academic year came forth with an all-encompassing plan to increase diversity at all levels of the university, called the *MSU Idea*. While the scheme is brilliant, its fault is that it is a scheme without a mandate for direct action. Plus, it lacks the appropriate allocation of monies to effectuate its immediate implementation. Instead of mandates to find, recruit, and hire minority faculty, departments are devising their own *MSU Idea* plans, involving a year-long planning and assessment process. These departmental plans are supposed to lay out the unit's goals, objectives, needs, and schemes for increasing minority participation at no specifically defined point in time in the future. This is literally an academic scheme; it does little to direct departments to move at deliberate speed to increase the participation of minorities, and rather provides an institutional excuse to delay positive action.

Similar grandiose schemes and tactics are being used at other institutions. A prominent tactic is the creation of a high level administrative position such as a vice president or vice chancellor for minority affairs and/or institutional diversity. These positions are being created specifically to buy the institutions time by hiring one more token "highly qualified" black to "coordinate the institutions affirmative action efforts and plans for increasing its institutional diversity."

The duties include (usually without a budget)

(a) coordinating the recruitment of minority faculty and students,

(b) supervising minority student organizations, and

(c) promoting activities and programs to increase the minority presence on campus.

Interpreted literally, this means providing the institutions with a built-in excuse and someone to point to a few years hence, when probably nothing will have been achieved.

In all fairness it must be stated, however, that some institutions are making legitimate efforts to improve the situation of minority access and participation. Where such instances are occurring, they are results of direct mandates and positive actions. One such instance is at Wright State University in Dayton, Ohio. Some three years ago the new president at Wright State directed the deans and department heads to increase the numbers of minority faculty, period. He also provided an incentive by directing that annual evaluations for administrators would include an assessment of their performance and progress in recruiting and hiring new minority faculty into tenure track positions. These administrators and departments who carried out this directive would be rewarded and those who failed would be penalized both in terms of budget allocations and personal merit increases. Using this direct mandate approach, 30 new minority faculty had been hired over a three year period ending in 1989 at Wright State University; about half of those were blacks. Progress can be made when there is institutional commitment.

Toward remedies and solutions

As we mentioned earlier, we have already learned enough to address the problems of black and minority student access and retention in higher education. There is hardly a pressing need for further extensive research in this area. Yet, there are still some specific research areas that need to be explored to enlighten and document some things we already know and some about which there are strong speculations. But the greatest need is for institutions to take what has already been learned and to act on that knowledge.

The American Council on Education's Commission on Minority Participation in Education and American Life in its 1988 report, *One-Third of a Nation,* challenged the nation's institutions of higher learning to "greatly expand their efforts to increase significantly the number and proportion of minority graduates" (p. 21), and offered a plan by which this could be accomplished that is worth repeating here:

1. Recruit minority students more aggressively at every level.

2. Create an academic atmosphere that nourishes minority students and encourages them to succeed.

3. Create a campus culture that values the diversity minorities bring to institutional life-- one that responds powerfully and forthrightly to incidents of racism that have occurred too often on campuses in recent years.

4. Place special emphasis on inspiring and recruiting minority candidates for faculty and administrative positions.

5. Work with educators at the primary and secondary levels to improve the education, training, and preparation of minority students.

The literature abounds with similar recommendations and examples of successful programmatic strategies that provide models for institutions to change the dreadful situations of minority access and retention. Despite this large volume of literature, institutions continue to disregard the need to seriously address these problems and to allocate the resources to increase the success rates of minority students. Part of this problem is the misheld perceptions that minority student retention issues center around academic inability and financial aid problems rather than the social, interracial, emotional, and institutional programmatic needs of these students that are not being met, especially at predominantly white institutions.

Scott (1989) has offered some enlightening recommendations for increasing black admissions and enrollment to colleges. Pruitt and Isaac (1985), suggested that institutions should:

(a) establish new recruitment avenues that reach minority groups, and (b) reevaluate the screening and admission process to expand the traditional criteria to include factors indicative of minority student success (p. 99), other than standardized test scores and grade point averages.

Such factors that have been found to be good predictors include leadership ability and participation in extra-curricular activities, positive self-concept, and the ability to recognize and cope with racism (Pfeifer & Sedlacek, 1974).

The increasingly scarce financial resources at institutions of higher learning has heightened the competition for these resources and dampened the enthusiasm of institutions toward establishing special retention programs to assist minority students generally and black students in particular. The prevailing attitude seems to be that after nearly 20 years of set-asides and affirmative action, the plight of blacks has not improved dramatically and now it is time for blacks to "pull themselves up by their own bootstraps," regardless of past and continuing discrimination. In order words, institutions want to bow out of the affirmative action business. Yet, it is recognized that institutional retention programs can make a significant impact on the retention and success of black students. What must be realized is that retention programs are most successful when they are institutionalized and institution-wide in their scope--that is, each academic unit must be mandated to assume some responsibility and accountability for retention.

Numerous institutions across the country have developed retention programs in recent years aimed toward improving minority student retention. The list is too long, and the specifics are too many to begin to discuss them here. Nevertheless, there have been many successes reported from these programs proving that they can be effective. Some examples have been reported in recent publications. What we have learned about these programs is that they must be tailored to meet the needs and situations of each institution's circumstances. While there are certain commonalties, such programs must be derived by dedicated administrators, faculty and staff who recognize the need and understand their own institutions (Lang & Ford, 1988; Ward & Cross, 1989; Richardson et al., 1987; Fleming, 1984).

We have learned that the situation of blacks in higher education is not a hopeless situation. It is a situation that is crucial and critical, and one that requires immediate national attention. It has been stated unequivocally and we have learned that the nation's response to the current crisis of blacks and other minorities in higher education will significantly impact upon and has serious implications for our future viability as a country and our future position and competitiveness in the world community.

References

Allen, W. R. (1987). "Blacks in Michigan higher education." In J. T. Darden & C. Mitchner (Eds.), *The State of Black Michigan: 1987.* East Lansing, MI: Urban Affairs Programs, Michigan State University.

American Council on Education. (1988). *One-third of a nation.* Washington, DC.

Ascher, C. (1987). *Trends and issues in urban and minority education* (ERIC/CUE Trends and Issues, Series No. 6). New York: ERIC Clearinghouse on Urban Education.

Astin, A. W. (1982). *Minorities in higher education: Recent trends, current prospects, and recommendations.* San Francisco: Jossey-Bass Publishers, Inc.

Center for Education Statistics. (1987). *Digest of education statistics, 1987.* Washington, DC: Department of Education, Office of Educational Research and Improvement.

Christoffel, P. (1986, October). "Minority access and retention: A review. " In *Research and development update.* New York: The College Board.

Fleming, J. (1984). *Blacks in college.* San Francisco: Jossey-Bass Publishers, Inc.

Gavin, J. R., III. (1989). "Issues and strategies in the retention of minority faculty and staff in higher education." In W. E. Ward & M. M. Cross (Eds.), *Key issues in minority education: Research directions and practical implications* (pp. 55-70). Norman, OK: Center for Research on Minority Education, University of OK.

Lang, M. (1986). "Black student retention at black colleges and universities: Problems, issues, and alternatives." *The Western Journal of Black Studies,* 10(2).

Lang, M. (1988a). "The black student retention problem in higher education: Some introductory perspectives." In M. Lang & C. A. Ford (Eds.), *Black student retention in higher education.* Springfield, IL: Charles C. Thomas Publisher.

Lang, M., & Ford, C. A. (Eds.). (1988b). *Black student retention in higher education.* Springfield, IL: Charles C. Thomas Publisher, Inc.

Lang, M. (1988, Summer). "The dilemma in black higher education: A synthesis of recent statistics and conceptual realities." *The Western Journal of Black Studies,* 12(2), 65-72.

Lang, M. (1990a, Forthcoming). "Barriers to blacks' educational achievement in higher education: A statistical and conceptual review." *The Journal of Black Studies.*

Lang, M. (1990b, Forthcoming). *The crises in American education systems: Implications for minority researchers in higher education* (1989 monograph series). Cleveland, OH: Center for Applied Research, Cuyahoga Community Coll.

Maguire, I. (1988). "Reversing the decline in minority participation in higher education." In *Minorities in public higher education: At a turning point* (pp. 25-44). Washington, DC: American Association of State Colleges and Universities.

Matney, W. C., & Johnson, D. (1983). *America's black population - 1970-1982: A statistical view.* Washington, DC: U.S. Department of Commerce, U.S. Bureau of the Census.

National Commission on Educational Excellence. (1983). *A nation at risk: The imperative for education reform.* Washington, DC: U.S. Department of Education.

Orfield, E., & Paul, F. (1987-88, Fall-Winter). "Declines in minority access: A tale of five cities." *Educational Record* (pp. 57-62).

Pfeifer, C. M., & Sedlacek, W. E. (1974). "Predicting black student grades with non-intellectual measures." *Journal of Negro Education,* 43(1), 67-76.

Pruitt, A. E., & Isaac, P. D. (1985). "Discrimination in recruitment, admission, and retention of minority graduate students." (Cited in Scott, op. cit., 1989). *Journal of Negro Education,* 54(4), 526-536.

Pruitt, A. E. (1989)." Access and retention of minority graduate students." In W. E. Ward & M. M. Cross (Eds.), *Key issues in minority education: Research directions and practical implications* (pp. 73-96). Norman, OK: Center for Research on Minority Education, University of Oklahoma.

Richardson, R. C., Jr., Simmons, H., & de los Santos, A., Jr. (1987, May/June). "Graduating minority students." *Change,* pp. 20-27.

Scott, H. J. (1989). "Issues in increasing minority participation in graduate education." In W. E. Ward & M. M. Cross (Eds.), *Key issues in minority education: Research directions and practical implications.* Norman, OK: Center for Research on Minority Education, University of Oklahoma.

Stamps, D. C. (1985). *Self concepts of ability, self-esteem, forces of control, and the perception of the opportunity structure as predictors of coping ability among selected black college students* (Unpublished Ph.D. dissertation). Hattiesburg, MS: Department of Educational Administration, The University of Southern Mississippi.

Tinto, V. (1975, Winter). "Dropout from higher education: A theoretical synthesis of recent research." *Review of Educational Research,* 45(1),89-125.

U.S. Bureau of the Census. (1985). *Statistical abstract of the U.S., 1986.* Washington, DC: U.S. Government Printing Office.

U.S. Bureau of the Census. (1987). *Summary characteristics of the black population for states and selected counties and places: 1980* (Supplementary Report PC 80-51-21).Washington, DC: U.S. Government Printing Office.

U.S. Department of Education. (1988). *Projections of education statistics to 1997-98.* Washington, DC: U.S. Government Printing Office.

Ward, W. E., & Cross, M. M. (Eds). (1989). *Key issues in minority education: Research directions and practical implications.* Norman, OK: Center for Research on Minority Education, University of Oklahoma.

Wharton, C. R. (1986). "Public higher education and black Americans: Today's crisis, tomorrow's disaster?" In *Minorities in public higher education: At a turning point* (pp. 3-20). Washington, DC: American Association of State Colleges and Universities.

Wilson, R. (1989). "Access and retention of minority faculty and staff." In W. E. Ward & M. M. Cross (Eds.), *Key issues in minority education:Research directions and practical implications* (pp. 41-54). Norman, OK: Center for Research on Minority Education, University of Oklahoma.

TEN TENETS

I Would
Impart to
African-American
Scholars

by
Mary
Howard-Hamilton

A common occurrence today is the presence of African-American scholars on our predominantly white campuses. However, very few scholars successfully complete the requirements for their degree. Concomitantly, African-American enrollments in graduate school declined tremendously the past decade. It was found that African-American enrollment in professional schools increased, but not enough to offset the overall loss beyond the bachelor degree level (Sudarkasa, 1988).

In 1976, Black undergraduate enrollment reached a high point of 10.5 percent of the national total, up from six percent in 1968. By 1980, it had declined to 10.1 percent, and by 1984, the last year included in the American Council on Education's *1986 Report on Minorities in Higher Education,* it was down to 9.5 percent. Between 1980 and 1984, the decline in numbers went from 932,254 to 897,185, representing a net loss of 3.8 percent. Blacks were the only major racial or ethnic group whose undergraduate enrollments declined between 1980 and 1984; other minorities and whites experienced an increase (Sudarkasa, 1988).

It is obvious that African-American students are encountering immense obstacles on our college campuses which impede their academic progress. Thus, I offer ten tenets to African-American scholars for empowerment, entitlement and strength.

Tenet One: Maintain a healthy lifestyle

If you wish to successfully traverse your domain and academic career, you must be a sound and rational thinker. Therefore, you must possess a sound mind in a sound body. A scholar who has a phenomenal physical make-up but a weak mind will be easily lead or directed by persons who may not be concerned about your best interest. A scholar who is a discerning analyzer, but is lacking physical strength will not be able to withstand long arduous hours of hard work inside and outside the classroom. Kondo (1989) stated that "a healthy mind prevents mental oppression." He also stated that scholars must strive at all times to strengthen and nurture their mental and physical abilities and capabilities. Drugs, alcohol, and tobacco products are injurious and should be avoided.

There are several ways to maintain a salubrious lifestyle. You can exercise at least three to four times per week for at least 30 minutes, take a daily walk, meditate in a quiet area and empower yourself with positive affirmations, write your thoughts and feelings in a journal, or write a letter to a significant other in your life. Browne (1978) stated succinctly that "if you stay healthy, both mentally and physically, you should have the energy and drive, the aggression and motivation to graduate from college."

Tenet Two: Establish and maintain a set of goals

There is an old adage that says: "If you fail to plan, you are planning to fail." Every African-American scholar must write down what they would like to accomplish in the next five weeks, five months, five and ten years. In order to accomplish your goals there are four main steps: Plan purposefully. Prepare prayerfully. Proceed positively. Pursue persistently.

A purposeful plan is one that has goals clearly stated and objectives listed to accomplish those goals. There is a purpose or reason why you are in school, perhaps to become a doctor, lawyer or educator. Know what your main purpose for attending college is, and be committed to it.

African-American scholars must have faith in themselves to accomplish the goals they wish to attain. Faith is inculcated in the scholar's cognitive domain by daily spiritual planning. This can be accomplished by reflective thought, positive self-talk, or communicating with a deity in your own way.

Self-sabotage, or listening to negative internal mental tapes, can impede your goal-oriented progression. Therefore, proceed positively with all

thoughts, deeds, and actions. Jensen (1987) says that if you encounter a temporary setback, mistake, or failure, "... pick yourself up and try again, using what you learned from your failure to increase your chances of success in the future." If you allow your mind to be tainted by negative thought, you cannot accomplish the last step, which is pursue persistently.

Be dedicated and maintain a tenacious focus when accomplishing your goals. Many scholars fail to achieve their goals because of procrastination. Rather than working diligently on a project, paper or assignment, many scholars will wait until the last conceivable minute and turn in a poorly-constructed piece. Scholars must be resolute and relentless in their pursuit for excellence.

Tenet Three: Be Mentored

An Afrikan proverb cited in Kondo (1989) stated that " The new broom sweeps clean but the old broom knows the corners." Your mentor will "know the corners." He or she will keep you appraised of significant events that could shape your life, offer advice as well as solace, be your confidant, and guide you in the right direction.

The following list (provided in part by professor Herbert Exum), describes pertinent characteristics and/or behaviors one should look for in a good mentor:

The faculty mentor should graduate several African-American students and/or students of color each year;

The faculty and/or administrative mentor should write articles with his/her students;

The faculty and/or administrative mentor should have a national reputation in his or her field;

The faculty, administrative and/or student mentor should be well respected in his or her department;

The faculty, administrative and/or student mentor should be well respected on campus;

The faculty, administrative and/or student mentor should be active in his or her professional organization;

The faculty or administrative mentor should be an advocate for African-American students; and

The student mentor should be a leader in his or her student organization(s).

The African-American scholar can observe and emulate individuals who have achieved their goals. Thus, mentorship is a positive vicarious learning experience. We all have had an individual in our lives who has always been an essential source of guidance (Kouzes & Posner, 1987).

A mentor can help you navigate the system, make important introductions, and point you in the right direction (Kouzes & Posner, 1987). However, what if you do not have or cannot find a mentor on your campus?

African-American scholars who may have difficulty in finding persons who fit the description provided on the mentor checklist may look to historical figures or prominent contemporary leaders for inspiring action (Kouzes & Posner, 1987). There have been many great African-American leaders such as Martin Luther King, Jr., Sojourner Truth, W.E.B. DuBois, and Ida B. Wells-Barnett. Read their biographies and study their leadership philosophy. Kouzes and Posner (1987) noted that "the next book you buy or check out of the library ought to be a biography of a leader you admire. Then make it a practice, one book a month for the next year."

Many contemporary leaders make audio and video tapes of their motivational speeches, as well as travel the lecture circuit. Attempt to rent or purchase a tape, or attend a lecture if they are in your area. Familiarize yourself with the list of "Afro-centric speakers" found in Zak Kondo's (1989) *The Black Student's Guide to Positive Education*.

Finally, you can also locate and interview African-American alumni who are working in your academic field of interest. Find out what steps they took to ensure their success. You can also learn first-hand from those you think are masters of the craft (Kouzes & Posner, 1987).

Tenet Four: Take calculated risks

One of my favorite quotations is by William O. Douglass, who stated that "the richness of life is adventure." A risk is nothing but an adventure or journey that will broaden your horizons and make you a stronger person.

A risk-taker is a prescient visionary, one who can foresee, imagine, and believe that they can overcome obstacles and make a significant contribution to society. Albert Einstein once said, "Imagination is more important than knowledge, for knowledge is limited to all we know while imagination embraces the entire world, and all there ever will be to know and understand." Therefore, to make well-calculated risks you must realize that life is an endless journey in self-discovery and personal fulfillment (Hatcher, 1986).

Take a risk by studying abroad for a semester or a year. If cost is a factor, become a national exchange student. Attempt to expand your horizons beyond the confines and limitations of your current institution. Become a cooperative education student and gain valuable work experience in your field. If you are an upperclassman, apply to graduate and professional schools out-of-state or away from your current institution.

By taking risks, you will expand your personal and professional network. When you become a risk-taker you will experience some dissonance. However, keep in mind that this form of healthy stress is important because it teaches you to assimilate and accommodate competing issues, values and alternatives. This makes you a better thinker, analyzer, and intellectual. The Holton Consulting Group (unpublished speech) postulated that "the two most powerful nations in the world are determination and imagination." Be a determined scholar and take a risk by doing something extraordinary at least once in your college career!

Tenet Five: Be willing to make a sacrifice

Sacrifice as defined in Random House (1968) "is the surrender of something of value for the sake of greater gain." African-American scholars must place materialistic wants and desires aside temporarily until their college education is complete. Kondo (1989) stated that African-American scholars must resist unproductive and self-destructive enticement. Many African-American scholars attempt to keep up with their peers or enhance their image by purchasing new cars or an ostentatious wardrobe when tuition bills and/or rent must be paid. It is obvious that this kind of individual is not willing to make a temporary sacrifice or surrender these materialistic goods for a greater gain--a career and future.

You will make many sacrifices in your college career (e.g. separation from a loved one, full-time to part-time job, less time spent with friends). Therefore, keep in mind that your college career is temporary and when you receive your diploma(s) you will be working for the next 40-plus years of your life, which is plenty of time to purchase the materialistic items you wanted. Enjoy the small sacrifice you are making because greater rewards are forthcoming.

Tenet Six: Practice and portray Afrocentric thoughts and values

Kondo (1989) listed several ways in which African-American scholars can become an Afrocentric scholar and educator:

Study Afrocentric educators who have your best interest at heart;

Study and learn an Afrikan language;

Study a map of Afrika;

Visit Afrika as often as you can;

Identify yourself first and foremost as an Afrikan person;

Support and celebrate Afrikan Liberation Day (ALD) and other events;

Honor the nationalist flag;

Celebrate Kwanzaa yearly;

Learn the Black National Anthem;

Take pride in being Afrikan;

Study your history; and

Keep up-to-date on the plight of Afrikans around the world.

With the resurgence of Afrocentric paraphernalia , medallions, Kinte clothing, and popular shirts bearing the *Black By Popular Demand* slogan to name a few, it is tantamount that scholars believe in the cultural and African-American attitudinal message they are portraying. It is hoped that what we are seeing is not merely a fad, but a positive change in the level of consciousness of African-American scholars.

Tenet Seven: Aspire to attain an advanced degree

When I was a junior at The University of Iowa, my mentor told me that "the only thing a B. A. means is Begin Again." I have never forgotten her words. She inspired me to complete my master's degree. Furthermore, I always knew that education is an arduous, continuous and lifelong process. I will always need to be educated and re-educated.

If African-American scholars are to be the next teachers, leaders, role models, and mentors, they must have academic as well as personal credibility. A graduate or professional school degree is a "must" for the jobs that will become available in this decade and the next millennium. We are in dire need of more doctors, lawyers, and educators. Charles Holsey (1990) commented that:

> There is already a shortage of Black professionals, and the forecast for the future reveals an even more

drastic decline. Imagine the year 2020, with the majority of the faculty at historically Black colleges and universities not being Black. Scary, isn't it?

Therefore, I implore African-American scholars to "begin again" because our future hinges on your academic success.

Tenet Eight: Know and love yourself

Would you be able to write down ten things you like about yourself in three minutes? If you know and love yourself this task would be a cinch to accomplish. As an African-American scholar, you should take the time to reflect on who you are, where you are headed and how you can co-exist in your current environment.

The African-American scholar must cultivate and hone two essential personality traits, confidence and tenacity. Knowing that you have the internal fortitude to complete a difficult task takes a tremendous amount of courage and confidence. You must know yourself and have faith that you can accomplish your short and long range goals. Concomitantly, if you know who you are and are not confused about what you are (Kondo, 1989), then members of the dominant society cannot attempt to devalue you or manipulate your levels of self-esteem.

Tenet Nine: Contribute to the body of literature on African-Americans

It is important for African-American scholars to publish poetry, songs, articles,and manuscripts about our culture. Many myths and distorted tales have impacted our knowledge base. It is time to dispel these myths and contribute positive research on the African-American. Kondo (1989) succinctly states that "communication is vital to our struggle." If you have an opportunity to write an honors thesis, master's thesis or dissertation, devote your research, in whole or in part, to the study of African-Americans. If you see an editorial or article written in the print media which portrays a negative image of African-Americans, write an editorial to refute the information. My mentor and doctoral committee member told me to "always question the truth, because it will withstand intensive inquiry."

Tenet Ten: Give something back to the community

This final tenet can be accomplished by an African-American scholar who is currently enrolled in college or after graduation. Make a personal commitment to accomplish at least two of the following suggestions:

Patronize African-American businesses;

Tutor an African-American high school student in your area of expertise;

Become a Big Brother or Sister to an African-American youth;

Devise your own list of tenets and teach them to African-American students in your area;

Present workshops and lectures on steps to success, careers, "how to get into college," or ethnic pride, to African-American high school students; and

Devote some phase of your life's work to the enhancement of African-American people.

Conclusion

The purpose of this "think-piece" is to redirect the thinking of African-American scholars, to get them to focus on how to empower themselves and successfully graduate from college, rather than to wait for the system to empower them (which will never happen). Celebrate who you are and understand that you hold the key to our future. Susan Taylor (1989) stated that,

Life should be a liberating experience, an exercise in self-expression. Ours is an open universe, offering each of us infinite possibilities. Hold on to the truth that you are human and divine, that you can realize your dreams.

References

Browne, L.F. (1978). *Developing skills for coping: For minority students at predominantly white institutions; but maybe for all students.* Unpublished manuscript.

Browne, L.F. (1980). *Midpoints vs. endpoints.* Unpublished manuscript.

Hatcher, B. (1987, March). "Let yourself go! " *Readers Digest,* pp. 169-170, 313.

Holsey, C.M., Jr. (1990, Feb 1). "Black America: Be patient with black graduate students." *Black Issues in Higher Education,* p. 28.

The Holton Consulting Group, Inc. (1990). *You can do it: Take it to the limit.* Raleigh, NC: Author.

Jensen, M. (1987). *Women who want to be boss.* New York: Doubleday.

Kondo, Z. (1989). *The black student's guide to positive education.* Washington, DC: Nubia Press.

Kouzes, J.M., & Posner, B.Z. (1987). *The leadership challenge: How to get extraordinary things done in organizations.* San Francisco: Jossey-Bass.

Sudarkasa, N. (1988)."Black enrollment in higher education: The unfulfilled promise of equality." In J. Dewart (Ed.), *The state of black America 1988* (pp. 7-2). New York: National Urban League.

Taylor, S.L. (1989, August). "In the spirit: Possibilities." *Essence,* p. 47.